LR

W9-CUF-292

MURDER AND OTHER ESSAYS

BOOKS BY DAVID ADAMS RICHARDS

FICTION

The Coming of Winter

Blood Ties

Dancers at Night: Stories

Lives of Short Duration

Road to the Stilt House

Nights Below Station Street

Evening Snow Will Bring Such Peace

For Those Who Hunt the Wounded Down

Hope in the Desperate Hour

The Bay of Love and Sorrows

Mercy Among the Children

River of the Brokenhearted

The Friends of Meager Fortune

The Lost Highway

Incidents in the Life of Markus Paul

Crimes Against My Brother

Principles to Live By

Mary Cyr

NON-FICTION

Hockey Dreams

Lines on the Water

God Is.

Facing the Hunter

DAVID

ADAMS

RICHARDS

MURDER

AND

OTHER

ESSAYS

DOUBLEDAY CANADA

Doubleday Canada and colophon are registered trademarks of Penguin Random House Canada Limited.

Library and Archives Canada Cataloguing in Publication

Title: Murder, and other essays / David Adams Richards.
Names: Richards, David Adams.
Description: Essays. | Includes poetry by the author.
Identifiers: Canadiana (print) 20190077786 | Canadiana (ebook) 20190077794 |
ISBN 9780385666558 (hardcover) | ISBN 9780307376077 (EPUB)
Classification: LCC PS8585.I17 M87 2019 | DDC C814/.54—dc23

"Playing the Inside Out" was originally published in *Playing the Inside Out/ Le jeu des apparences* © 2008 by David Adams Richards. Reprinted by permission of Goose Lane Editions

Jacket design: Andrew Roberts
Jacket image: Echunder/Shutterstock.com

Printed and bound in Canada

Published in Canada by Doubleday Canada, a division of Penguin Random House Canada Limited

www.penguinrandomhouse.ca

10 9 8 7 6 5 4 3 2 1

Penguin
Random House
DOUBLEDAY CANADA

This book is dedicated to my late friend the poet Eric Trethewey, and my sons, John Thomas and Peter Anton, with much love.

IN MEMORY OF ERIC TRETHEWEY

You phoned the last night you were alive
To ask if we could take a drive
Into New Orleans sometime.
I said yes, let me first get to Virginia.
You who could be as fierce as a pit bull
Left abandoned,
Or as gentle a poet as God intended,

Never quite understanding the world
Where you seemed suspended,
Fumbling for keys to some kingdom
Controlled by a sombre attendant.

When Kelly phoned the next day
To tell me you had gone,
Found dead on the floor of your kitchen,
I remembered how the phone had
Rung once more that night later on.
"Oh," I said to Peg. "It's Rick again—
I will talk to him tomorrow."

The best of us are left fumbling for keys
To doors that remain locked
On this life we borrow.
This poem
Is addressed to you, my friend
For your courage, love and sorrow.

CONTENTS

ESSAYS

A NOTE FROM THE AUTHOR

Some of these essays were written thirty-five years ago, some just this year. Some have previously appeared in newspapers and periodicals, and some have not. Most have not been previously published, though I did have a short book of essays published in the 1990s called *A Lad from Brantford*, and have taken a few essays from that.

Playing the Inside Out was formerly published in book form by Goose Lane. I have included some poems. These also span nearly three decades and most have not been previously published.

MURDER

IT WAS A JULY NIGHT AND I WAS TRAVELLING HIGHWAY 11, along the Miramichi River in northern New Brunswick. Along the way I picked up a hiker, coming from town. It was dark and warm, and the stars seemed endless; endless enough to make us reflect that anything we did couldn't much matter to the wide universe. And this in fact is what the hitchhiker reflected upon as we drove.

That we didn't matter very much at all.

So I agreed. (It is a fairly prevalent idea nowadays. It is part of the irony of the times, I suppose. That is, that any office or opinion we have is, by way of irony, lessened; and nothing much matters.)

He was a nice fellow, a First Nations man who was travelling home to his reserve. I believed he simply wanted to make conversation. "Dust in the Wind" was playing, a song by the group Kansas—their lyrics stating that all our dreams are futile, for we are only dust in the wind.

He concurred. "That's right—boys, oh boys, look at them stars—people think we matter, but we don't matter much—"

His voice belied the import of the statement, making it homey and wise and innocent.

I agreed that when you consider our galaxy and try to comprehend the billions of others, you realize we are very tiny indeed.

However, there was something else I had noticed. It gave a curious feeling of aggrandizement to say we didn't much matter—a feeling of actual importance in not mattering. We felt enlivened by the prospect that we were nothing. For a while it filled up a need in us. In fact it must have filled up something to be able to say it with so much contentedness.

Infinitesimal specks of nothing that we are.

The hitchhiker said after a time that he was an atheist. That he had become one because the church had hurt his people.

"The church turned me into an atheist" is what he said.

The song had stopped.

I did not dispute this. That the church—and many other things—had hurt and displaced his people. He was telling me now that he was not a Christian and did not believe. I shrugged. I was not in the mood for an argument. And it never much mattered to me what a person is or was. That in fact is my stance, and always has been, and too, at times, I am still not certain what I am.

Still, I began to realize that in saying we did not matter because there were big stars in the sky, we offered some kind of acknowledgement to at least one line: "For as heaven is above earth so are my ways higher than yours, and my thoughts than your thoughts."

I was reminded of this as my friend spoke, and wondered if I could convince him of its veracity. Because I had gone through at least a few of the same things he had. Not to change his opinion any more than my opinion.

So for argument's sake, let's say the line is true—that as heaven is above earth so is Christ's thinking above ours. That would put us on the plane to use a scale—of, say, a snail. (Just for argument's sake.)

As heaven is above earth so is our thinking above that of a snail (I am not intending to cheapen the snail by saying this). However, be that as it may, we still look upon a snail as pretty important. We do not want the wilful slaughter of snails. Or at least most of us would frown at the wilful slaughter of snails. Some of our more conscientious eco-activists would say, in a perverse way, the snail is rather more important than we are.

What does this have to do with my First Nations friend and me driving alone at night, on a secondary country road, with a mile or more between houses?

Quite a bit, actually.

If Christ's thinking is that far above ours, are other lines Christ uttered true also?

Well, to put it all in some context, likely they are; and very likely they were given to us to reflect upon and keep with us no matter what.

So then let's acknowledge another line:

"Even the hairs on your head are counted."

Or

"Not a sparrow falls that isn't known."

Studying these lines, do we see a contradiction with the immenseness of Christ's thinking? Or do these lines support his reasoning?

That is, if even the hairs on our heads are counted, do we matter if the universe is so vast?

Well, we must matter a little for even the hairs on our heads to be known enough to be counted by someone whose thinking is as vast as the universe itself.

This in fact is what my friend and I had dismissed a few miles back. And both of us were pleased in some way that we had.

But as my new friend spoke of his life—and it was a horrendous life—it made me think of these two sentences spoken by Christ, about the hairs and the sparrows. For when my passenger spoke in his Micmac accent, he spoke of a humanity that had betrayed him, and yet his voice was still filled with disarming gentleness.

He pointed to a star and asked, "So then—who is their God?"

But what he was actually saying was—we were so tiny no God would bother caring about us. That is, that the tininess caused our insignificance to God. That is, he was saying even if a God did exist, we were too tiny for him to care about.

Many scientists would be willing to say the same: that the universe is so grand that we do not matter. A scientist might then point out star number 9020—and smile at our stunned embarrassment over her brilliance; because she can show us a wobble or a shadow and tell us a planet exists 204 million light years away, which then proves how insignificant we are.

But after work, when this scientist is in her own home deciding how to prove 9020 matters to her own inestimable work and the research grant she desperately needs, she comes very close to saying that both she and the star 9020 matter very much. So if she matters, the planet she is rotating on must matter somewhat, as well.

And in fact she is right—for I am sure, to take a leap of faith, she was meant to find that wobble and was meant to determine how incredibly important it is. And I believe that it was known by some universal force she would discover what she discovered when she did.

If we talk about sparrows and hairs on the head, et cetera, we are speaking of something very important: the sanctity of life inherent in the count, and our own lives as being sacred. And in some way it must be true—for why would Christ ask us to think of our lives in these particular and peculiar minuscule terms unless it was to instruct us about something very important?

I mean, wouldn't we think of more significant things about ourselves? Our strength, our wisdom, our beauty? We should not be thinking of little hairs at all, should we?

But this peculiar notion of what to count is in every way an exquisite judgment not only about us but about the world, the universe and the wobble.

That is, if Christ's statement about hairs on the head was frivolous, we would all soon recognize it as frivolous. He would have been laughed out of town. But if the hairs on our heads are counted, we can be assured that everything else about us is counted, as well.

But I think this is a more important matter than just one of what is being counted. For isn't Christ's message meant to be much more—an actual psychological transference from our own small physical realm into some far greater existential plain of cosmic awareness? Why else would it be said the way it is said if this was not true? Is it the cosmic awareness of Christ, and the awareness of our own link to the cosmos, that Christ is asking us to contemplate in one single hair?

So when Christ said this two thousand years ago, wasn't he giving us a glimpse into our divinity, and to the nature of the entire universe, by using a hair?

And if the physicist Leonard Susskind, in his argument with Stephen Hawking, is right about black holes, he has said almost the same thing: that no information is lost, that all information about our universe is somehow not destroyed or forgotten, at the event horizon.

In effect, was Christ not telling us this two thousand years ago?

This gives us a primitive glimpse into our nature, where we in fact do measure up to the galaxies, the universe and the wobble.

To make us holy or to see the holiness attached to the augment that is "ourselves"—even if it is only for the briefest of moments in our lives. That is, though we might go days or months without thinking of the hairs on our head or our arms, tiny and transparent in the sunlight, once we realize this about ourselves we *have* realized it. And Christ wanted us to realize it! So then is this an *affirmation* of Christ? That is, we affirm the genius or the greatness or the transcendence of so many others—can we at least speculate about his greatness by saying that his observations were if not holy, which I believe they were, then at least profound? That is, I have always argued from this point. If you cherish the thinking of Aristotle then you must Christ as well. And Einstein himself would be the first to tell you so. For even if you think he is not divine—he is such a profound thinker no one in the world should ignore him.

The First Nations hitchhiker was very happy to get a drive. It mattered to him that he did. So he mattered very much, and so did the hairs on his head, and it becomes more significant as this story goes on—so mattering is relative to the circumstance we are in.

After a while I was not so sure we were right a few miles of dark secondary road back. That is, perhaps we weren't meaningless—and the ability to look at these wonderful stars actually proved it. For perhaps something far greater than ourselves allowed us this glimpse.

The road we were on wound its way through spruce and over small bridges, a single lane of asphalt highway that for anybody from a city would seem the edge of the world. But a world I have lived in most of my life.

My Micmac friend had just gotten out of jail a few hours before, and he told me he was going home to do a job. He was very charming in a self-effacing way.

"How could any God care about us—my life is nothing," he suddenly said.

Of course I told him he mattered.

He shrugged and said that I did not know him or his hardship. So for a while we were silent.

Yet I thought, if our world is an insignificant blue dot at the tail end of the Milky Way, why is our dilemma never an outward one but an inward one? As his seemed to be at that moment. Why was he so riled at the world he had just called nothing at all and quite unimportant? And why was everyone else's dilemma much like his—that is, an inward one?

Is it because everything else in the universe is concerned about the same things? That is, that someday we will come to know that our universe is an ethical, moral and spiritual universe and nothing more than that. Or I should say nothing can be greater than seeing such in the universe; and it is a very false idea to think the universe proves that the moral and ethical dilemmas we struggle with daily are not important because the universe is so vast. That vastness does not matter in the least. That in fact the Spaniards going west to the New World thought it as vast as anything could be. It did not transform them. Neither did it transform the Dutch, or the English or French—all of them at times acted horribly in the name of king and country.

And the First Nations people they met on the way used torture and mutilation in the same self-serving manner. So one may come to think in examining this that our world lacks all basic principles of goodness. And you would be right, except for one thing. Looked upon in hindsight, we see what they did was appalling and an affront to humanity. We know this not because we have been told it was wrong but because we know in our hearts and minds it is wrong. That is, taken away from the self-aggrandizement of the moment, the moment always shows itself for exactly what it is, or was, and nothing can ever change that. Murderous behaviour will be seen for what it is. No one can hide from it. Not even the hair on one's head plucked out will be dismissed at the event horizon of a black hole.

If it was wrong then, and good people knew it was—it is wrong now, and good people know it is. So we know what is right and what is wrong, even if wrong takes over—and we know it whether we live here forever or travel to the ends of our earth or galaxy. We know in our hearts and minds when something is wrong. It may take hindsight to correct our vision, but our vision will always be willing to be corrected in the search for goodness and justice. And what is important here is this: our vision will always be willing to be corrected. For if it was not—if it was not willing to be corrected, then hardly any of us would be living now. So then there is a true point on which our vision should focus—and that is, that every hair is counted.

All of this had nothing to do with the moment, or everything to do with it, depending on where you sat.

For my friend suddenly told me what he was struggling with.

He mentioned that he was on his way home to kill his cousin. His cousin was a nice guy, he said, pretty handsome, had all the women—"And I like him a lot," he confided.

But he maintained he would have to kill him.

And I suddenly realized this was why he chose the topic he did earlier. For if he believed that we are in fact nothing—or that nothing mattered in the world, what would it matter if he killed his handsome devil-may-care cousin?

Well, it wouldn't—or didn't. But then, I replied, "Why should you kill your cousin—if we do not matter and we are nothing, then you are killing something that does not matter and is nothing, as well. Why bother with it at all?"

Because, he answered, his cousin had done something to him—he had stolen drugs, and his son, who was an addict, was now dead. So it was imperative he do it.

"I may as well go down tonight and get it over with," he said.

So I was in a bind. And I tried to think my way out of it. And in doing so, his moral dilemma suddenly became mine. But there was a subtle caveat—he had to convince me of his quest—and if he couldn't convince me of the nobility of his quest, he was willing to be talked out of it. But he needed to be convinced. Did I think he was bluffing? In some way it would never have mattered if he was. But I do not think he was.

So we returned to the argument. On the one hand, he said, his cousin was a good guy, a charmer—he was also nothing, and because he was nothing, he said he deserved to die. And I was merrily going along with his plan—unwittingly driving him to do the deed—until now.

"Death is nothing," he said with a wise sniff. "It wouldn't matter to me if I die—so why should it matter to him—you know what I mean."

"Not exactly."

"Well—it doesn't matter one way or the other." He shrugged. "Life isn't that important—we just have to look at the sky—just specks—"

In fact I now know this rationalization has to happen in order for *any* murder to be committed. The act, for at least a moment or two, has to be looked upon as not a crime but the removal of a person so worthless she or he does not matter. So then the idea that the hairs on this person's head do not matter is also a consequence of this deliberation; and what Christ said about them becomes a strange fallacy. No—more than a fallacy, an annoyance. For if they are counted, they matter; and if they matter, so does the person in question. So Christ could not have said what he said to tell us anything serious, so we can deny it is serious—and in denying what he said, we deny him and all else that he said. And every action we take that isn't in line with this thinking disavows his testimony. And this is what Christ warned us against, didn't he. Some will say the denial of him or his testimony is no longer important.

Well, there is something that proves them wrong. Exaltation in my friend's face at the moment he disavowed anything but himself.

The exaltation, comes from our very trivializing of what Christ intended by what he said, and our breaking of the promise God made to us when he said, "Thou shalt not kill."

Acting with self-will against this decree proves to me the very existence of God—for there is not another entity, force or person we are disobeying. Nothing else in the world can make us feel such disobedience as this crime, done against something we now must say does not exist.

There would be no argument at all if this was not really the case. Murder by its unnatural self-aggrandizement is in a strange way proof of the existence of God. For each of us knows in our heart we are breaking a law, beyond man's own law.

I mentioned a promise in God's law. So then, what is the silly promise he gave us? Is "Thou shalt not kill" a promise? It does hold us back when we have a club in our mitten. However, it is a promise in this one way—if one follows this law to its maximum, it applies not only as a decree for this man but as a promise of safety for this man's cousin.

We understand that if the law is followed, the cousin is safe. So the law is a promise to mankind. However, the buildup to acting out this ultimate sin often becomes a matter of pride or honour—and though we are reminded in a thousand ways that it is wrong, we have put so much faith in our pride and honour that we are incapable of saying no to either. And the feeling deep within us that it is a sacrilege and a crime against God's law allows us for a time this feeling of invincibility.

But who am I to say that? I am filled at times with remorse for my own past—my years of drunkenness, my own violence. So who the hell am I—

Well, I was one thing.

I was the person who was there to tell him not to kill.

I have in my lifetime known over a dozen people who were murdered and it has struck me that all murders essentially follow the same pattern; the ability to haul the wool over one's eyes in order to perpetrate the crime is the reason self-righteous justification is always a key ingredient. In fact, as I wrote in my book on faith, *God Is.*:

The self-righteousness of sin . . . is its main gloss, it is the veneer which soothes us if we wish to change the meaning or intent of what we have done [or what we want to do] in the eyes of others. It is far worse than hypocrisy, because it goes deeper into man's ambivalence toward truth. Or, in fact, supports our constant craving to change truth.

Hypocrisy knows the truth, and acts against it out of self-will, weakness, or desire. Self-righteousness bends the very idea of truth to accommodate a sin we can champion as being justified under the circumstances.

I suppose all this is known. But it just never seems to be known well enough.

The cousin was not important, my fellow traveller said. And he said it very often.

But I knew something about it. The real secret is: the reverse of that statement is always true. To the perpetrator of murder, the victim is extremely important indeed, and the perpetrator self-important. It cannot be otherwise.

And the more innocent the victim the truer this is.

My friend kept returning to the statement we had initially agreed upon. That we were all nothing—only dust in the wind. But now I was challenging this. So an argument started that was at times, in the dark cab, a little unnerving.

"But if we are nothing, and it doesn't matter, why would you do that?" I asked again.

"Oh well, it don't matter—that's why I am doing it," he responded. He then reflected on how he would do it.

An axe, he decided. Then no, he did not care for killing people with axes.

He looked at me curiously and asked if I hunted.

"Yes, I do hunt," I said.

"You wouldn't have a .30-30 on you?"

"Not handy," I said.

Then he would have to burn this man out, he explained, because the police had taken all his rifles. So the house would have to go, too.

A big old blaze—right on the shore. A bonfire! he exclaimed.

He pondered this and wondered where he would get gas. Well, he would not get gas from me—even though he seemed to be hoping for my support.

But I suddenly thought of something.

"Are there others in the house?" I asked. There was a long, almost embarrassed pause and finally he confessed this to me:

There were probably his cousin's children at home, Tina and Fred.

"My God," I said, "Tina and Fred—well, you can't just up and kill Tina and Fred."

"I am not after them," he said, as explanation.

"But you do not want them to come to harm, do you?"

At first he said it did not matter if they did. He shrugged and put his foot up on the dash, and sniffed and lit a smoke.

He said he couldn't help it if they were there. It would not be his fault if they were. "Anyway, why would they be home?" he said.

"Okay, how old are they?"

"Five and nine—"

"Well then, maybe because it is close to one in the morning and they are five and nine," I answered.

We were silent for almost a mile.

"What do you want me to do about it?" he said. "It's not my fault they are there."

"Well, you can help one thing."

"What is that?"

"You can help it that you are there."

He was silent and shrugged.

He said that he did not want the children to come to any harm —is that what I thought of him?

"Not at all," I said.

"Well, I don't," he said.

"Then you should let it go." I shrugged, too—as if this were a normal conversation, as if we were in deciding the fate of children simply talking about the timing and logistics of it all. "So that tomorrow night they can see all of these stars, too—"

He laughed suddenly. I was glad of that. He said I didn't know what I was talking about. He said nothing mattered. He began to play with the radio, trying to find another station.

I realized in some way all people who consider murder are in many ways like Napoleon, who said, "Men of my stamp do not commit crimes."

That is, all men for a moment think that they themselves are absolved from the idea of the very crime they are going to commit. Later—when they run away and hide—as Tolstoy said Napoleon did on his retreat from Moscow—the true nature of what they have done catches up with them.

I let him off at a side road some miles from his destination, knowing that he would be safe on such a warm night, and he would have much time to reflect. I turned the truck around and went home. I was going to call the police and was certain I would.

But for some reason I did not. So I sat all that night wondering if I had done the right thing.

The hours passed. I sat at the kitchen table unable to sleep. Or even to think very well. I wondered if he had gotten another drive, or if I should go and see where he was.

The moon was high over the trees, the stars were everywhere, and a sheet of white informed me of the Milky Way. I finally fell asleep at the table just before dawn.

The next day there was no report of a calamity anywhere. It was a beautiful day, and there was dew on the leaves when I walked down to the brook. I sat there all day thinking about what to do—but again I felt he would not do it. And that night, once again the stars—a billon of them—flooded the heavens.

And another night passed away, and then two nights and then a week. I still worried. A month went by, and then two. Then he was arrested, this fellow, for something else. Later, after his sentence was served, he returned to the reserve. But he never harmed the cousin or his children.

This happened fifteen years ago. In the blink of an eye the years have passed by.

His cousin and he are now both dead, gone to their rewards by natural means—and the children are grown up. And that long-ago night is remembered by me, at times of reflection about chaos. And I think often about the reasons for self-justification, murder and the sadness of man's tragic heart. And what saved us was a child's head lying on a pillow, in that ramshackle house.

For in the end it did matter to both of us, as much as anything else in the heavens, that Christ told us the hairs on our heads were counted and known.

2009

CALIGULA, LEGERE AND
THE NATURE OF POWER

YOU'RE WALKING HOME—FROM A TAVERN—A BIT DRUNK. YOU'RE singing a song you learned when you were in the navy ten years before, making up some of the words as you go.

It is a winter night—all the streetlights are out. You don't have much money. But what you have you've promised to bring home to your wife.

Just as you approach your street, you see someone standing alone off in the dark. He jumps you and tries to steal your last few cents. You fight back. But suddenly you discover who it is.

You're so stunned that you let go of him and he runs off down the alley clutching your money in his hand, his toga flying, his spindly legs in their strapped leather thongs and his balding head visible under the cold light of the moon. He makes a dash around the corner and is gone.

The year is AD 39, the place is Rome under the consulship of the young emperor Gaius Caesar (Caligula)—and you've just found out the hard way that the lad is bonkers. Is so much of a loon that he hangs about Rome at night to mug his own citizens. Some say it's for kicks, because he had nothing much else to do—others say it's because he loves the smell of money. (What's wrong with that?)

But what's worse is that you have to go home and explain this to your wife, who's been waiting to buy some bread and salt. Who in their right mind would believe a story like this?

Gaius believed he was a god—and the son of a god—and, as the historian Suetonius tells us, he had his palace extended to the temple. Had the heads removed from various statues of the various gods, and had replicas of his own head put on. He became, in a way, all gods.

He would walk around and pray to himself, or ask himself favours.

"Rise me to heaven or I'll send you to hell," he is reported to have told one god.

Others, as well, believed that Caligula was a god. He could, in fact, do anything he wanted. So perhaps it's farfetched to think of an actual emperor, who could do anything he wanted, coming out of the darkness to mug you. (Imagine the likes of a president doing such a thing.)

Gaius's ascension to the throne after the reign of Tiberius—a man so strong he could put his thumb through a boy's skull if he wanted, and sometimes he wanted—was viewed as "a real dream come true."

Except people found out they couldn't mention goats in front of him. No goats. Because by his mid-twenties his head was balding, and he felt the mere mention of a goat was mockery against him. So he'd have your tongue taken out.

You had to crouch down when you passed him, somewhat the way Groucho Marx did, because Gaius couldn't stand anyone taller than he was, looking down at his bald spot. So people would, on pain of death, lower themselves about a foot when they went by:

"Bear in mind I can treat anyone exactly as I please."

For some reason that rarely meant opening the granary.

He was said to have sawn a group of theatre goers in half for not proclaiming him an immense genius after his first stage production. (I see no difficulty here.)

Horror, of course, is somehow always funny in hindsight. I have known people to have laughed themselves silly over disembowelment. (However, not their own.) Perhaps it keeps us sane.

And Suetonius makes no great distinction between Gaius's victims being chopped up or disembowelled, or merely having their throats slit for sneezing at a party in his honour, as had happened to certain little boys.

"Suffer the little children to come unto me" was not a big line with Gaius. It is an exceptional idea that Gaius was alive, not much more than a child, when these lines were first offered. Also, it is an exceptional idea, perhaps not consciously intended by Suetonius, that all evil is the same, and hatches the same crime. That the acts are different in different places, but that in fact there is only one evil perpetrated against the world, constantly and always, and forever the same. That they are continually linking together like a giant DNA to form the one monstrous complexity of deceit.

All crimes essentially are formed within the same framework and have one body. And all those who suffer from the pieties of power and empowerment are suffering from the same crime.

Those who suffered under Caligula are the same as those who suffered by the hand of Miramichi serial killer Allan Legere.

Legere's sniggering as he washed the Downey sisters' blood from his body is the same sniggering Caligula afforded his entourage. It cannot possibly be different.

Suetonius talks about Caligula mocking Claudius, as well as having an old man dress up as a gladiator to face an equally decrepit lion (as you can imagine, people were rolling in the aisles over this one) to cutting the tongues out of knights, and slaughtering children.

As he tells it, it all seems to be the same sin.

Now, whether Gaius was mad because he drank out of one-too-many lead goblets, who's to say. There were more than enough lead goblets to go around, and not everyone proclaimed his horse a senator. "Let them hate me as long as they fear me," he often said.

"If I were you, I'd fear me" I remember Legere telling a boy at the pool hall one summer day in 1966.

Gaius made the court philosopher Seneca the brunt of his mania often enough. Until Seneca wisely noted:

"No one can instill fear, except in the amount they have in themselves." This is appropriate not only for an emperor but for a small-time hood, as well. It is not one iota different.

Gaius must have had some fairly lonely nights, when he was not stealing his friends' brides at their weddings or hopping in bed with his sisters.

He must have realized on those brief excursions into the dark, as he saw his reflection in the ditch water, that madness isn't entirely the fault of one's stars.

And finally, like Legere, he must have understood that he only thought he was in control.

"I can do anything I please" must have on occasion sounded hollow to him. For it must naturally be followed by "What else can I do?"

(Funnily enough, these are very comparable to the lines Legere is reported to have uttered at his capture: "I could have done this—I could have done that. My name is Allan Legere.")

Neither could ever seem to do enough. Both were self-agitated by inner loathing. Eventually Caligula was murdered in his garden. His wife and children were murdered shortly after that.

Although Suetonius calls Christianity a "mischievous sect," and categorizes Gaius's persecution of the Christians as one of his good acts, there is some comparable reasoning with it.

Suetonius, like Saint Paul, is too observant not to see the toadyism of high culture and false humanity, the rancid perfume that covers up the vomit of vanity.

Suetonius tries to let us understand these men in physical terms, because he wants to warn us "that their bodies are their limitation when compared to some greater idea." And this is what we come to realize again and again throughout history. That the torture chamber and the knifing on the side street show that power always leaves out the greatest ideal.

Suetonius's fault lies in his problem of not really knowing what this greater ideal is. He knows there is one—he knows the emperors should have it. He is unsure as to why they do not hold it.

He does not know that the very thing they have limits their ability. Power eclipses the one idea that surmounts it: humility.

Yet he allows us to understand, in his great two-thousand-year-old book, that the power of Gaius is not much more than the power of Legere when looking down from the stars. And hell walks in Little Italy wearing a two-thousand-dollar suit.

The inescapable dilemma of all men and women is that they need to use whatever power they have to prove again and again to themselves that it is theirs.

1993

SMOKING

I BEGAN TO SMOKE AT THE AGE OF THREE, WITH MY FRIEND Kenny, under the veranda of his house, about the autumn of 1953.

We would crawl behind the steps, squeeze our way under the veranda and light up our first cigarette of the day—which was ten minutes after our mothers scrubbed and dressed us, fed us and threw us outside for the morning.

My memories of those children are faint and distant, and are that they were always dressed in bright colours as they walked along the paths between our small white houses.

There was always the smell of wood and smoke at night, and the smell of earth. There were ships in at the wharf, and old men still wore Humphrey pants. Sometimes they had a good pair of Humphrey pants along with a regular work pair. The women wore long dresses, and some women had a mink collar on their winter coats. The radios were still as large as one living-room wall: TVs were a rare commodity.

Kenny's mother's purse, black and aristocratic looking, sat upon the counter, with its package of Export sticking out the top of it; sunlight coming through those old venetian blinds in the corner.

The thieves I knew then were young enough to have a sense of hilarity about their vocation. Gain was nothing without the hilarity attached to it.

As soon as his mother began to clean the house, Kenny would go after those cigarettes with a bravery most people only admire from a distance.

I suppose today he might be called "slightly hyperactive." We would soon be out the door and under the veranda and lighting up. We would sit back against the blackened brick foundation, and stare at the floor of the veranda—puffs of smoke seeping through the cracks in the boards—and look through the latticework, to watch my grandmother come around to the coal chute; or watch the milkman standing on the veranda above us, wisps of smoke about his feet.

Years have passed, and you know, almost half of the children I grew up with are gone: booze in cars going too fast in the night, or some other sad assault upon the body. Those brilliant and wonderful children I still see in old photos, standing in the schoolyards in the snow.

No cigarette has ever tasted better than the ones I had when I was three and four. The smell of tobacco in the tight paper, mingling with the smell of autumn burdocks scraping the side of the wall in the cooling wind—was, I suppose, as close to purity as I will ever know.

The trouble was Kenny didn't think so.

It is a fact of my life that I have often been close to people who will *never ever* leave well enough alone—but who, for some peculiar reason, have to continually *tempt* God. And worse still, bring me along—as in this instance—as a sort of burnt offering.

It isn't that Kenny lit me on fire right away—but I did notice him becoming more and more remote—as if he were drawn to some other purpose his mere two-and-one-half-foot best friend in the world couldn't comprehend.

And never minding all the times he reprimanded me for letting too much smoke go out through the slats or squeeze up through the boards and rise toward the milkman's knees, he suddenly took it into his head to smoke on the street by the pole—leaning up against it, just once, like the adults did, with our ankles crossed.

So one morning that's what we did. We walked out of our hiding place with fresh cigarettes in our gobs, like tiny Humphrey Bogarts, and walked right into the arms of my aunt, who was coming down the sidewalk.

"Is that a cigarette?"

I shook my head—as if it wasn't a cigarette.

"My good *God*," she said. "I'm telling your mother."

"She knows I smoke," I said.

This was the first of two or three sentences my aunt and I ever exchanged.

Of course I was lying. I had not really told my mother yet. And anyway, my mother was standing out on the porch at that moment.

I don't think I would have smoked so readily after that day if it wasn't for Kenny.

Time passed. We smoked in fields, and when snow fell and made the ground ash white, we smoked behind the fence that separated our property. Long ago, we puffed in the sheds across the street, and sitting in the gully, with cigarettes in our pockets and tucked away in our mittens; and when we couldn't get cigarettes, we rolled up newspapers and put leaves in them. And once when we couldn't find a pole to stand beside, we smoked in a hole dug for one, leaned up against the shale rocks and crossed our ankles.

And though we thought we were well hidden, as children always do, we must have been in plain view to grown-ups half the time—because always we were caught, searched, scolded and forbidden to do it ever again. And grown-ups were continually sniffing us up and down—twice a day, at least.

These were the same days as when another little friend of mine jumped off the roof of his house using an umbrella as a parachute, and a young woman—younger than I am now by twenty years—had an infant who was dying, and would stop Kenny and me on the street, as if by talking to us she was somehow able to ease her pain. Nor did I ever feel she wanted other adults around when she spoke. But too often we were trying to hide cigarette smoke when she came to see us. And I never knew her name; remember now only one thing: that her soft wavy hair was brown.

But these in truth are my first few unclear memories of what became a near-lifelong addiction. (I have finally managed to quit.)

Another memory is the movie.

Kenny and I were staring at Rory Calhoun, and Rory Calhoun was lighting a cigarette off a stick he had taken out of a fire, while he leaned back against his saddlebags after a hard day's ride.

And Kenny came to some conclusions about how we should smoke from then on.

We would go home, he said, and build a fire in his backyard, heat the sticks and light our cigarettes from them. We would, in essence, have a permanent supply of matches.

No one would see the fire, he explained, because we would build it so close to the house—right near the oil barrel—that it would be hidden from view, and we would never let it go out.

Kenny never thought the fire got out of hand, even when my coat sleeve lit up as I was dipping a stick into it. Never once was he daunted in his effort to light a cigarette like a cowboy. Even when he was being hauled away, kicking and screaming, by his mother.

The wall of his house was seared for a year with a burn mark that rose to the kitchen window in the shape of a spruce tree.

The oil barrel was drained and carried to the basement.

Kenny began to carry a silver cigarette case about with him— who knows where he got it: sometimes there were even cigarettes in it. And he began to puff on his father's cigars whenever he could get his hands on one—and invite me over when his parents were out and Charles, his brother, who was supposed to babysit him, was playing road hockey.

His mother threatened to send him to a home—where the Jesuits would take over. That was the most common threat in those days.

"I'll send you to a home and let the Jesuits take over." But she never quite had the heart to.

So it was close to Christmas 1954 that Kenny lit the couch in his house on fire with a big White Owl cigar. He had crawled behind the couch to light the cigar, and puffed away solemnly, not realizing that the tip of the cigar was burning against the couch.

He barely escaped alive.

They dragged the couch outside and let it sit in the snow and mud, upside down.

I don't remember Kenny's father very well, but his plan seemed ingenious. He went to the store and came home with a pack of fat White Owls. And then they tied Kenny in his high chair. Then they handed him matches.

"Here you go," his father said. "You little bugger—smoke them all."

It is what was once known as "aversion therapy for addiction." An arcane and cruel method of dealing with addicts—and, back in the 1950s, in its infant stages—which is probably just as well.

"See, you'll soon get sick now," his father said. "Smoke them all—you'll see."

They stood about the high chair glaring down at him, while Kenny, in weary compliance, struck his first match.

After a while the rest of the family sat down to breakfast.

At that moment Kenny's aunt drove into the yard. All the way from Nova Scotia. Came for a Christmas visit and wanting to surprise them. She walked through the door. Everyone happy to see her, the baby nonchalantly flicking the ash from his cigar with an experienced finger.

"My God, Jenny," she said. "I didn't know the baby smoked."

I lost touch with him when I moved to the other end of town. As over the years I have lost touch with so many of those children I knew and grew up with, and loved in my youth. But from the age of eighteen on I never opened my third pack of the day without cursing him a little.

I finally went cold turkey, and have come to blame my years of smoking on my own weak will and bad character.

However, if anyone would want me to describe sainthood, I might have to consider Kenny the day I went to visit him while his brother was out playing road hockey.

It is all in the way you perceive how a child of three smokes a cigar.

1986–91

LITERACY

I SUPPOSE, LIKE SO MANY OF US, I DID NOT THINK MUCH OF reading when I was a boy. I know there are those who always had that inclination, and that is a good thing; and no doubt with that inclination there were parents who encouraged it, and that, too, is a good thing. And though I had parents who did encourage learning and school work, I did not really begin to read until I was fourteen years of age.

The book was *Oliver Twist*, and was given to me by a friend for Christmas, and I remember thinking when I looked at it that I could never read it because it did not have any pictures. And who would put a book in my hand that did not have at least one or two? At any rate, some months later, sometime in March, I did pick the book up after it fell from my night table, and I began to read. I finished the book in three days.

At that time I decided two things: I decided that Dickens was a great writer, and that I wanted to be a writer, too.

There was one remarkable moment in that text that when I read it, I realized that yes, not only is that exactly true, but the exact truth must be sought, understood and known, and if known it should in some way be imparted to others, and in imparting this we must do it with compassion and understanding. That is what that sudden moment gave me, and it changed my life—or at least the direction of my life—and made me realize that without compassion there was neither understanding nor truth.

You see, what that moment revealed was the soul of a boy—not Oliver, but some other orphan on the street—and gave us a certain knowledge about his tragic little life, through empathy and love. For the rest of my life, or at least for the rest of my life until now, I have been obsessed by that perimeter, and a needing to testify about it, if to no one else in the world, then to myself. It was only a single line or two in a book that has long since been misplaced, but it indicated to me a part of my nature that until that moment I did not know I had. Or if in fleeting moments of my youth, I knew I had, I didn't measure the consequences of having it. But it also allowed me a mirror into the souls of men and women—and Dickens when writing those lines in 1837 could not have imagined that a boy reading them in the spring of 1965 would be so overcome by this that he would relate it to you in the spring of 2018. The souls of men and women were sacred—that is what Dickens was saying.

That is why Tolstoy, who said one could see the heavens in ditch water, also said that all the mad and overwrought characters of Dickens were his friends. Because Dickens showed us the template of goodness in human beings—a woman named Nancy, hardly a saint, and many times a thief would die protecting a child from Bill Sikes; the Artful Dodger and all the irascible crew of little lady and gentleman thieves who could never read or write and who would suffer penury or death in the workhouses of London, or be forced into hard labour or hanged by the neck until dead at the age of nine, were still protective of one another and the orphan Oliver. This was the soul and it had nothing to do with reading, except in reading was revealed to us. A rather strange counterbalance in life. It made me realize what I had realized as a child: that all people were in fact important—why I found solemnness and goodness in the most unremarkable and derelict of people.

For you see I already knew these people. I had seen them on the streets and embankments of my little town. Girls like Nancy and men who had suffered through neglect and war and drink. I knew the rich middle classes, too, and a cross-section of society that middle-class suburbia never experienced. So I knew these people, too, in my heart. Yet in a way it did take a book to allow me to realize it. What does this have to do with literacy? In a certain way everything. For not only did these Dickensian children never have the means to read or write, even where I grew up in the fifties reading and writing to broaden souls was in some ways discouraged by many.

And worse there were times growing up that I saw those who knew how to read and write use it to triumph over others, never to help them. That is the conceit of learning that we must all be aware of, the haughtiness of a degree, which has nothing to do with what a degree is for. It is why I have loved all my life the boys and girls of the street more than the boys and girls of the classroom. It is why I have sat with men who have no education more than with those who have. But I have also seen in them the struggle—like the man who spent his life in the woods and was terrified to take his firearms acquisition test because, though he had hunted and guided from the time he was twelve, he could not read. And he whispered this to me as we sat side by side. So a friend of mine and I managed to tell the forest rangers his predicament, and they allowed him an oral test. For you see, in the woods and on the rivers that man who couldn't spell *woods* or *rivers* would outshine us all. Let us understand this now and forever. Or the young man who did not want his wife, who was discovered to be exceptionally bright, to go back to school, because he was afraid she would become educated and leave him. And how frightened he was when he spoke of this. And it was out of selfishness, yes, but it was also out of loneliness, forsakenness and love. For he himself had never learned to do what she was now being given a chance to.

Therefore I know the boys and girls of the classroom have a great duty—like a writer or a politician; a grave duty to help those who have been denied access in whatever way to the classroom itself. Shame on us if we do not recognize the obligation. But shame on us, too, if we ever think a labourer as that young man was is less than a professor.

I remember when I was a boy, my first time in Toronto, and I saw in a restaurant a group of students from Osgoode Hall making fun of a waitress who did not understand their big words. Nothing showed less kindness or understanding of responsibility to the human heart than that. There are two things detrimental to the human soul: ignorance coupled with arrogance, and knowledge without compassion.

It would be fine if those who have knowledge always made a point of understanding compassion. Years ago children who had nowhere to go in summer lined up to put their names down with my friend Helena Waye, a teacher at their elementary school, hoping for a chance to go to summer camp, where my son worked.

Some had never been to a place where they could canoe or swim. And because the list was so long, many were not picked. And every day from April to June they would ask her, "Am I going to go, too?"

Dickens wrote a story about workhouses and pickpockets in the spring of 1837. If it had been just a story about that time and place, it would have had little to say to a boy in the spring of 1965, and less to us in the spring of 2018. But in a way it sanctified them, made us realize they were a part of us, now and forever. Hopefully we take this with us, no matter where our authors come from or our individual education demands; hopefully we take this, then, no matter what part in life we play, and realize that the greatest part is to be both generous and noble, the greatest part is never to leave others out, or behind, but to realize as they are loved and sanctified we are loved and sanctified, too.

2018

WE TOLD THEM THEY WERE BUILDING A DREAM

A FRIEND OF MINE VISITED FROM THE MIRAMICHI TWO DAYS ago, bringing Christmas presents for the kids. He is up here, in Toronto, working a shutdown. That is to say, he's a man who goes into a plant when it closes for repairs and does repairs, a travelling troubleshooter of sorts for industry—in this case, American industry, Chrysler or Ford.

He has been doing this now for twenty-five years: away from home, seasonally, for a generation. He has raised his family this way. The copper-zinc mine he used to have a steady job at, on the Miramichi River, closed years ago, when he was much younger and far wilder. Well, he can still be wild. Enough to make many turn pale. Yes, they'll never take that away. But I often wonder if he ever thinks of the cards life has dealt him. His marriage is over, in part because of his travels—yet he needed those jobs to pay the bills.

The fishing is gone on my river, the mines, too, and the lumber industry has been hit blows that would stagger Jake LaMotta.

Another mill has gone down this month—UPM from Finland; six hundred more men. It becomes, after a while, just another statistic.

My friend is just one of the hundreds of men (and women) from Miramichi, New Brunswick—home of my great river—doing this now: travelling for dignity. In a real way, as clandestine as it seems to people who might not know, these men from all parts of our country are still the backbone of the nation. You meet them in places they never thought they would have to go. You can tell by their eyes, in a second, that they are the ones to keep Canada going. They have worked shutdowns and drilling operations and pipelines; in the woods and on the water; have repaired everything from heavy equipment to sewers to hydro, and travelled to Quebec during the ice storm, or to British Columbia during the fires, and helped keep people alive.

To say these men didn't have proper life skills or training—which might be said by some—is as silly as saying executive management of the nineties should have known a company was going to be downsized; or a professor was silly because he wasn't offered tenure, even though he was as capable as anyone in his field.

The Miramichiers believed, too, in the industry they were trained for.

They are millwrights and boilermakers and mechanics, lumbermen and heavy-equipment operators. They married and had dreams, and kids and houses and jobs. There was nothing wrong then or now with the skills they acquired. They simply need to travel farther from where they belong to use the skills they have. And now they're growing old.

They leave their families behind in order to send money home. They spend months in single rooms, sleeping and working, and keeping children's birthday promises and spouse's anniversary dates by email or cellphone. So the problems with substance abuse and broken lives won't be mentioned here.

The real secret is the damn mill was never ours anyway. That is Canada's true tragedy, which goes beyond my region.

This time, the company was Finnish. It could have been from anywhere. But whoever owned it, they were dealing with people they didn't know, or ever feel obligated to. Our natural resource was all that mattered. The sanctity and security of our life didn't matter too much. In fact, the Finns are still cutting the wood as I write this. They will just ship it to other places for processing. That is a cynicism and disrespect to our people, not only by the Finnish company (in the end, who gives a fig about them?) but by our own government. Come to think of it, it is *never* morally justifiable to lay all the blame on outsiders.

So the people of the Miramichi are kept afloat by the Alberta tar sands. The men I know, many old school friends of mine, and their sons, have gone out. This is what keeps our towns and villages going this Christmas Eve. For the entire substrata of our economy, the shops and stores and appliance dealers and property owners, depend on a world that has crumbled beneath them. The men have gone away—and send money home to keep the region alive.

It's been almost fifty years since the great Escuminac fishing disaster. On June 19, 1959, thirty-five men, drifting for salmon in Miramichi Bay, were drowned in the most violent storm to ever hit our water. On that desperate night, men gave their lives for their friends; boys no older than fifteen made sure their little brothers and fathers were saved before themselves; small boats turned back into the teeth of the storm, and refused to abandon those in trouble.

When asked about it, one fisherman said, "What in hell else could we do?"

I am sure the men leaving everything they have known to provide for those they love say the same thing now.

2007

NORTHERN NEW BRUNSWICK

HERE WE ARE A NATION, A SMALL ONE TO BE SURE. BUT THAT IS not surprising.

Our ancestors. They are the ones who are buried here, in graveyards that look toward a sea.

There are no bathers on the grey stone beach today—our majesty isn't found in the hot sun or burning wind, though both do come. On a beach as grand as any, the sand dunes are swept and the yellow grass stings and cries.

Berries look adolescent most of the summer and ripen suddenly. Our men pick with the women.

Few rent houses. When a young couple get married, they build their own. There are many fine and modest houses, but there are curious-looking ones, also, sometimes propped on logs, sometimes finished only long after the family has moved in—when a family builds its own house, friends help with a neighbour.

There is always a road, a highway. We live beside it.

So our beauty is rough. It has shades like the soul. There are always fishing boats. There are always fishing men, lobster boats, drifters, trawlers. And the sea. It has become a part of the Acadian language, this water, the occupation.

When Acadians say goodbye, they reflect their heritage poignantly. What they are really saying is:

"I'll hope for you."

In English towns the small United, Presbyterian and Baptist churches lie white and smooth in the afternoon, reflecting the heat and the sun on their windows. In the white pines that tower above them you hear the trees talking to each other. Here there are gods.

One only has to breathe the air to appreciate them. No wonder the Micmac thought us blasphemers.

Twilight reflects a gothic world in the woods where the roads have been beaten back and water trickles into the shade.

To youngsters who have grown up here there is always the sense of wonderment just before dark.

"The Browning" the Acadians say.

In the summer, I grew up where the night came as solid as a stone. It had the blackness of a full tide in the dark.

Only a few small cottages gave off their light, and far away a buoy or now and then a beacon from across the bay, that was seen only at night.

There are distances that are mysterious and primeval to the young. The smell of water, the spruce are stunted by the salt wind, the grass turns white and curls inward like hair, close to the bay, and inland barns can be forgotten for a generation, only to be discovered, explored and claimed by the young. The sun burns on their salty backs, and their eyes reflect the icy waters.

Fishermen don't sunbathe or carry radios and blankets to the sand, nor for that matter oil themselves with suntan lotion. Many can't swim, and never have. They don't think of the summer for beaches or brown tans. For the fisherman there is always something akin to deceit in that form of supplication.

When they drift for salmon, they are gone all night. There are always legends. And when I was young, I heard the sea all night and knew what those legends were.

I would not hear the sea now as I did then—for the gift only comes to the young and stays only as long as he is willing to remain under the spell.

Here our triumph—and tragedy—is living in a land that contains so much power. It is not the tragedy of Greece or Rome, or Arabian nights. Theirs, as Camus has said, is beauty. Theirs is also its pints of gold, its sheer tragic need to be happy.

Under a blanket listening to the night sea the young never feel the need to be happy. Our stories are not of genies found in a bottle on a beach shining with emeraldic power in a land that is both distant and sad to the tale teller. We are too young for such legends. Ours have human blood: animals known to us by touch.

Water that we've seen.

Our bay is blue-green, and I'm often reminded of my early years when I smell tar. For there was tar on all our wharfs.

When the sunbather was on the beach, he was safe—he was afforded a respect. There was no quarrel with him. Let him lie upon a blanket and soak up the sun, and worship it as he would. Take radios if he would.

The very young never lie on the beach for more than a moment. The very old have no use for it, either.

It is only for the idle and, in respect to so many things about the sea, the idolatrous. Let sun worshippers cringe when I say this.

I don't imagine the sunbathers happy, for I've seen greatness in the fisherman's eyes. This is a personal observation, one that comes with the territory.

When the worshipping is over and the sunbather invades the wharf, then he loses his advantage. He is a sorry spectacle, out of place amid the true mirth. He becomes at once in his bathing suit and sandals, a derelict. No one intends this. It is universal law.

When the sea spoils and rises against itself, there are no swimmers. There are no windsurfers. There are fishing boats.

"The poor fisherman."

"The ignorant fisherman . . ."

I've heard jokes like this about them, so I mention it now. It shows the soul of the joker. There is always cowardice in their reflection.

As a sunbather cannot see beyond the first buoy, so he cannot know the sea.

"I'll hope for you," the wives and loved ones say.

That is, I'll hope not for your catch so much as for your return.

Though I'm sure there are some, I've never met a fisherman who didn't care for the cleanliness of his boat, or his house; who didn't keep things in order, and order within reach.

I've heard the stories. There were those who didn't come back. There have been boats found running and no one aboard. Everything was in place. The boat cut the water silently. All had the quiet of the swells, and the faint dimension of death.

It might be observed that no one thinks of fishermen dying until they do. Strange. It's as if they went to an office in the morning.

I know a man who lost two uncles to this bay and owns his own boat. He leaves land at five in the morning and his wife expects him at five in the evening.

I've never once seen fearless eyes except in those who have faced danger. To lose fear, a philosopher might tell you, is to have faith.

No one is prepared to die. To die for someone else, shows that you understand, even in terrifying circumstances, mirth and spontaneity. Not that you are mirthful, but that you have been.

There are gods in the wind, too, in the salt air. They are here in the middle of the summer, anointing those who can sense them.

Thirty-five didn't come home one night. The storm has been assimilated into our thought, and I mention it only briefly.

Men in the water having been tossed lifelines handed them to their brothers. It took one man half the night to reach land, and yet no sooner was he safe than he turned his boat back into the storm to help a friend whose boat had floundered.

A man tied his son to the mast, and then before he could tie himself was swept overboard and disappeared.

Boats—and you must realize how small a drifter can be in waves of seventy-five to eighty feet in height—refused to leave other boats in trouble and time after time threw lifelines, and shouted encouragement and kept watch.

So until the end.

These men have a genius for deflating their own heroics. They can do it by exhaling smoke from a cigarette and looking away from you quickly. So one must not intrude upon their thought.

Our gifts, our legends are as in every responsible nation—our own. We have breathed them into our blood.

They are physical presences in a room.

We meet them on the stairs.

1983

THE *SHANNON*: A SHORT STORY

Thirty-five men and boys were lost the night of the Escuminac disaster, June 19, 1959. This is a fictional story about a fictional family. But the heroics of that night can never be adequately recounted.

THERE WAS NO THOUGHT OF THE STORM WHEN THEY WENT OUT from the timbered wharf, starting the *Shannon*'s engine, an old Chevy that he and his father had refitted, putting new rings and gaskets in, an engine his father had bought second-hand from the *Lorrie Jane*—therefore as the older brother said had seen much of the bay's salt water wash over it already, across the gunnels in a spray. The older brother had never seen his father get a deal (except winning a Saturday-night bingo once).

The older brother had been the boy his mother had relied upon. People said he was the reason they had to marry.

The older brother had always worried about his dad. He walked out in a blizzard one night when he was ten, looking for him because he didn't come home. The only reason he had found him was that

45

he had noticed the red woollen bob on the top of his father's old woollen hat sticking up from the snowdrift. He dug his father out of the snow tears freezing on his face.

"Dad," he said. "Dad—please, Dad—wake up, Dad. Dad, please."

The older boy had been the one to try to find the money his father had won at bingo but had left in a shed at the wharf. It was a lot of money for them—seventy-eight dollars. The older boy never found it.

Sometimes his mother would say she was going away. The younger boy would hang on to her suitcase crying.

"Mom," the younger boy would beg. "Mom—please, Mom."

Besides, she had no money to go.

His father and mother always relied upon the older brother. He cut wood, banked the house, fixed the water pump and gave his savings to his dad, to refit the *Shannon* because his mom had asked. They were reduced to eating lobster, putting cardboard over the windows so no one would know. It was said that the older brother had saved money from haying and drifting for three years. He was going to go to university in Chatham.

Still, without the *Shannon* what would his father do? Then what might happen to his mother and his younger brother if he just left them like that?

"Think of him," she whispered, like she was praying. "Your dad is a good dad—I know he will prove it to you someday."

There were very good men here, men the older brother sometimes helped with their nets—men who kept their lives and their boats in order. His father had been in Korea in 1951, where he was hit in the head with shrapnel. His father never spoke about it to anyone.

The older brother counted on his fingers the money he might have left if he helped with the engine. His lips moved silently as his mother watched him.

"Someday you will know—I promise," she said. "He is a good man."

"I know, Mom. I know," he said. "Okay, Mom—okay—yes!"

She patted his hand. She seemed worn out by life.

It is not at all remarkable to those who know life that when the older boy thought of his father, his heart still filled with love.

If anyone recalled, the older brother was a thin young man, pale as a ghost most of the time. His smile was somewhat hopeful, as if he longed to fit in. He had black hair to offset such pale white skin, and people noticed—especially the girls—that he wore the same jacket and boots three winters in a row, and his hair was so black that it looked as if he wore a splash of tar on his head. Sometimes people would see him late at night, walking alone in the cold because his father had gotten angry and put him out of the house. Very late after his dad had finally fallen asleep, he would make his way home.

His mother didn't know that the older boy had had a chance to work on the *Lorrie Jane*. The captain of the *Lorrie Jane* put his arm on his shoulder and smiled at him: "You could work out with me if you want—if your father's boat is down."

"But what about Dad—please—could you take Dad on, too?"

The captain of the *Lorrie Jane* said he couldn't afford that. Neither could the *Silvia*. But the boy knew they were both frightened of his dad. That so many people were.

Later that afternoon he noticed his father and his younger brother trying to lift the old engine off its mounts.

And he went to the *Shannon* and said, "Dad—let me help—Dad—Dad, I am here—here I am."

So he gave his dad the money for the second-hand Chevy engine.

He was the one who broke his hand when they were mounting the engine, and it hadn't as yet mended.

Still, just after refitting the *Shannon*, his father started to have blinding headaches again. Many days he sat outside on a kitchen chair, with half the stuffing out of the upholstery, a bottle of Napoleon wine at his feet, and wouldn't come in to supper. Not much could be said about these headaches. He sat in the waiting room of Dr. McKenzie's office all day long. But he knew no one now could take the headaches away. They would only go away on their own. Except that when they went away, his father could always be certain that they would return.

So his older boy took a plate of food out to him that pulpy warm day with wind from the southeast. The older boy was very proud that day. He wanted to show his father his report card.

But his father couldn't read. He had gone to school until grade four and whatever he had learned he had lost as the years passed by. Now the boy mentioned for the first time that he was going to university in the fall.

"That's something, isn't it?" his father said.

The boy told him the priest (the same one who often came to the house to bless the rooms and speak to his father about trusting Providence) said he would be accepted at Saint Thomas. He did not tell his father that he had spent the money he was saving for university on the refitted *Shannon*. Or moreover that he had a secret to tell but he was going to wait until graduation.

His father nodded. They were very silent for a long time because his father had no idea what to say and they had been clumsy with each other a long time now. So his dad told him to take the younger boy, twelve, with him, to help lay out the massive gill nets that would stretch behind them. It would be a clear night, without much wind, and try to keep out of the shallows.

"I can't go tonight," his father whispered, "my head's very bad again. You'll have to take your brother."

His son looked at him. His dad's three-day beard was grey in small spikes, his eyes though still light blue were misty, and the hat pulled up on his broad forehead showed a strand of sad greying hair that seemed to rustle in the sudden wind and make him look boyish. Still, everyone on the wharf and everyone in town and anyone on the river knew he was no one to fool with. All the men knew that. His hands were large, his body was still very powerful, and he could stand the cold on the boats wearing only a woollen sweater.

"Sure." The boy shrugged. "Sure, I'll take him, Dad. I'll take him. I wanted to show you my report card is all. I'll take him. But he sometimes gets seasick—I mean, if there is a big sea."

"No, they tell me it'll be a clear, soft night. And I promised he could go. Here—" And he handed his older son a quarter. "Buy you both a treat for the night," he said. And he smiled proudly.

Then a small tern took to the sky, and they watched as it skimmed back along the shore, going toward the wharf where the drifters were tied.

His father noticed his son's hand wrapped in its cast. The cast was dirty enough, however, to show the hand must have almost healed. He looked at the report card his son had so proudly brought to him, but as always he couldn't understand what it meant. Then some tears flowed down his much-weathered face.

"What's wrong, Dad?" the older brother said, startled suddenly. "Don't worry, Dad—I'll take him out. I'll get him an Oh Henry! bar—he likes them."

The younger brother thought it would be like the year before, when he went out with his dad and lay across the housing, staring at the million stars in the warm night. That night as he watched his dad and older brother haul the nets, he felt very special, loved and cared for, and they cooked a salmon. Then just at dawn, or about dawn, they saw, he and his dad, the eighteenth-century English man-o'-war off on the horizon. His dad convinced him he had seen one of Wolfe's own ships moving up toward Quebec. It was always riding the waves its sails unfurled, his dad had told him, sometimes in the dawn, sometimes just at twilight, off far to the west.

This mirage was seen by many fishermen over many years, and must have been a ghost ship from long ago, his father told him, suddenly giving him a quick, innocent smile.

That is, this younger brother, who I met in university years later, didn't remember his dad like his older brother had. He told me that sometimes he would run into his parents' bedroom and see his father curled up on the floor. He would rush to the sink and put a damp facecloth over his father's forehead so his dad wouldn't have to grab at it. His father told him that when his head bothered him, it was a big gold nugget—and that someday it would come out of his nose, and they would be rich. Then he would buy their mother everything she ever wanted—a dishwasher, too. So, he told his son, if he yelled at night—don't be frightened, it was just the gold nugget.

"Sometimes your brother and I argue—but you know it means nothing," he said.

By then everyone, myself included knew that his father, captain of the old *Shannon*, had suffered a head wound in Korea and at times everyone was frightened of him. We knew that the older boy kept care of his family even to the point where he hid them in a special place when his dad was angry.

"My brother remembered all the bad times, so I would only remember the good," the younger boy told me. He was twenty when we met, and we were attending Saint Thomas University together. Oh yes, the younger boy knew by then that there had been no gold nugget, only a crude, heavy metal plate.

But it was I who revealed to him something he did not know. All these years later he didn't know it.

That is, that his father had fought hand-to-hand combat on a hill in Korea.

When the Chinese commander yelled, "Canada boy, tonight you die."

The few Canadians had yelled back, "Come and get us, you sons of bitches."

That is what had really happened to his dad's head. The younger boy did not know that. But his older brother always did.

There were nine hundred Chinese soldiers, attacking a forward position of twenty-eight Canadians. Running out of ammunition, their father had to use his flare gun to kill a man. And he finally fought hand-to-hand while having suffered a severe lacerated wound to the head. That he survived, they said, was a miracle. But his head would never be the same. The older brother knew this. And because of this he would never leave his father. The older brother often said, "Okay, Dad—it's all right. I'll go look for it."

Often his dad worried because he had lost all the bingo prize money that he had promised to take home to his wife. Even three years after he lost it, he would become agitated and sometimes he would wake his older son at two in the morning and ask him if he found it yet. That is when the neighbours saw the older boy walking outside. They just never knew what for.

The younger boy knew what had happened that night on the *Shannon*, though. He knew that they had gone out with mild winds, and laid down their nets behind them. But as night came on, it was not at all like the year before. Darkness piled over them, and he felt the hard wind pick up, the sea became unsettled and his brother had to bail, while the younger boy tried to help, putting the Oh Henry! bar back in his pocket. Then the waves started to hit the starboard side and the boat listed, righted itself, and the prow sank and came back up, as if the old *Shannon* itself was heroically trying to keep them safe, though he could hear the planking crack. The older boy realized with the water coming over at every wave bailing was useless. It would take everything they had not to be swept overboard.

He turned to tell his younger brother to seek shelter in the cuddy, and he would haul the nets, start the engine and start for shore. But before he could get to the cuddy hatch, a huge wave hit his brother hard and he fell back against the portside gunnels.

"And that was when you discovered your dad was aboard?" I asked.

"Yes—my father must have boarded when we were up on the wharf talking to Mr. Doucette—my father had come on, and was laid down in the cuddy all this time with his head throbbing. But then, feeling the sea beneath him, he came up. He took one arm and grabbed me, and with the other caught my brother—then, putting us back against the wheelhouse, he took an axe and cut the nets free. If not, we would soon have been sunk at the stern. The *Shannon* came up level for a bit and my brother, who had gotten the engine started, turned toward the shore."

"But your dad said you wouldn't be safe in the shallows."

"'No,' he said calmly to my brother. 'Boy, the shallows will kill us—if we have any chance we have to stay out.'"

His father was able to grab a bumper tire from the side and burn it in the little stove to keep the young boys warm. He told them he would get them a treat when they got home. Now and again he covered them with his own body. He took off his coat and put it over the younger boy. But everything got worse. At some point the mounts broke, the pistons were flooded and the engine went dead. A sudden eerie silence was forced upon them in the howling gale and the wash. The younger boy covered in his father's coat realized the *Shannon* was doing all it could to stay up. He saw lights and other drifters tossed like corks. He saw two men being swept away from other boats. He heard the shouts for help. And their father desperately tried to restart the engine to help another boat in trouble. It did no good. For the *Shannon* only had moments left itself. Every time the *Shannon*'s prow went down—every time the young boy thought they would drown—the *Shannon* came up again and rocked and struggled to keep them safe.

The father was silent most of the night but only said words of encouragement.

And for the first time in memory he kissed them both. He stood as the waves washed over him, his sturdy legs shaken but time and again reset. Until he knew there was nothing left for the tired *Shannon* to do, and he must lash his boys to the mast and pray to Providence as the priest had said.

The father didn't tell them he believed they were doomed.

How the young boy thought of his mother and how he would give her the biggest hug when he got home.

Then suddenly out of the gloom and off to starboard—it was just dawn by now—they saw the great wide prow of the *Silvia*—a drifter some ten feet longer than their own—coming toward them in the gale. Coming to rescue. But the waves were so strong their father was afraid they'd be washed over.

So his father grabbed him and lashed him to the mast. It was then the younger son got to see his father's face, as if for the first time. Only for a moment, mind you, for there was a great flash of lightning. His father's face seemed to glow with a kind of passion, a certain undeniable tenderness. And even at this desperate moment it made his youngest son smile.

But when his dad went to grab the older brother—the brother who had tried all his life to keep care of the family, the *Shannon* gave a groan and seemed to list over sixty degrees before miraculously righting itself again. Like a great dying friend, it came level with a great wash of water.

But the older boy was gone. Swept off the port side. He did not cry out—but the *Silvia* turned toward him.

"They'll never be in time," his father said. And he kissed his younger son, and he took the length of rope he was going to use to tie the older boy and dove into the water after him.

"He must have known it was useless," the younger brother said, remembering it with tears. "I thought of my older brother as being so big compared to me—but now I realize he was small and thin and gentle. He was like our mom, made for study—he was not made for the sea like my father or me. That he did it only because he loved his dad. You see, my older brother could not swim. That's how heroic my older brother was—no medal would be enough, I think.

"My dad tried so damn hard to reach him. To do so he had to let go of the lifeline he held. The rope was firm on the *Shannon*'s stern and Dad could have made it back. It was either the lifeline or my brother and I could see he almost made it—he was no more than a foot or two from him—but he had to let go of the lifeline. And he did let go. Almost with disdain he tossed it away. I saw it like a black shade in the morning air. But he reached my brother and held him above the water in his powerful arms for as long as he could. I think the *Silvia* might have gotten them if he could have lasted just a little longer. But then I guess he just couldn't do it anymore. The *Silvia* came back, and a man I didn't recognize came aboard. Ten minutes later I was aboard the *Silvia* and I saw our little *Shannon* go down. The *Silvia* circled for a long time, a long time, looking for them. But they were gone. My mother had walked down to the wharf and was waiting with so many others, wearing my brother's old coat, a housedress and worn black sneakers.

"My brother would have had his tuition paid for and a lot else. He had a Beaverbrook scholarship. That was a very big deal in 1959.

He whispered it to me that afternoon when he bought me the Oh Henry! chocolate bar. That's what he had told me—what he had wanted to tell our dad. But he said he would wait awhile longer. For a special day. When my dad no longer had a headache. Then on that day we would all be happy, my brother said. My brother was always my hero, I guess.

"And my dad. For you see, in the end my dad never lied. He did have a gold nugget. It wasn't in his head—I know that now—I know that's where all the pain and sorrow were, all the sudden flashes of despair—but the gold nugget was there, too, wasn't it. My brother always knew it. It was in his heart."

2017

CHILDREN

SOMETIMES THE MORE INSTITUTIONALIZED THE REASON FOR A
picture of children, the more it shows the children whole enough
to accept their fate. That they will endure their immediate circumstances knowing, or at least believing, things will be better.

A parade up a church aisle long ago, for First Communion; or an
exhibit of photographs about orphanages in London, England, in
the 1880s before those small orphans, the Home Children, entered
ships to be sent off to Canada and Australia.

Little Emma Cook, age four, holding a second-hand doll, on her
way to Canada. Or a five-year-old named Tom with one leg missing, standing on crutches, smiling, as if someone had just revealed
to him that he would be sent off alone to Australia and he said,
"Australia, sure."

When Saint Paul spoke about enduring all things, he spoke about
children.

And when he spoke of hoping for all things, he spoke of children.

Any Kool-Aid stand will tell you that.

Perhaps no one could imagine how hard Jack London worked when he was a child.

Or care, really, except as a way to change the laws.

The one thing children rarely exhibit is the self-righteous opinions that pretend to come on their behalf. I am saying laws that *pretend* to have the child's interest at stake.

Joe Louis at one time took on the work of the other boys around him because he knew they were not strong enough to do it: moving crates and ice blocks, at eleven years of age, up tenement stairs.

Many of my uncles and my wife's uncles worked in the woods from the time they were twelve and thirteen and took home less money in a day than you or I would now pay for a cup of coffee.

And one of the poorest boys I knew went to work for two years in order to get enough money so both he and his brother could start university together.

The practice of the chimney sweep that William Blake wrote about is long past, where little boys of five and six were known to have smothered inside chimneys they were cleaning.

But at least some of the opinions of our day are probably as intellectually deceitful as the kind that allowed chimney sweeps; or, for that matter, allowed boatloads of orphans like Emma Cook to be sent here from England in the 1880s. And come from the same mentality. It is what Dickens's fictional Oliver Twist had to face growing up in the 1830s: the demagogy of an adjustable social program. A program that is always scaled for people we consider beneath us but that we refuse to admit we consider beneath us.

Children have often been used as poker chips in the game of self-seeking, so much so that even the pictures of starving children create a degree of cynicism that no new diet fad could match. And allows us to vent our arguments against the children themselves. Just as a teacher might say to a school kid swearing, "I've heard all the words, boy," so have I heard all the arguments against children— or for children, but only the *right kind of children*.

Most of my friends, especially those of university background, believe it only appropriate and considerate not to want children, except under the right conditions. (Yes, and they know what these conditions should be.) Childlessness for the good of society is thought to be a radically new concept. (Supposedly, people like Princess Hélène in Tolstoy's *War and Peace* could not have thought like this.)

For instance, I have not been to a dinner party in the last twelve to fifteen years (no matter what organized religion, in no matter what region of the province) where the topic of unwanted children as a terrible societal problem did not come up. Usually sanctimoniously, or pejoratively; usually halfway through the meal. Once to explain her point a woman held her hand to her heart and proclaimed, "And he *swore* at his child." And she closed her eyes in virtue.

"Oh my," another said.

Well, full disclosure, so have I—and tell me I do not love my children. And tell me my children do not know this. To argue, and at times angrily argue, with your child is supposedly not to love him. Nonsense.

Still, for thousands this proves children are unwanted and unwanted children become a problem and a social issue.

Although what was and is camouflaged is the fact that when you talk of children as a problem, the last thing you are doing is taking the child's side.

Yet at these parties the argument is often that we are now, as never before, a very sensitive people who find it inexcusable how the world treats children, so it is best not to have many of them around. Of course there are women and men who will always be counted on to make fun of it all, glibly because they have been taught to react this way.

So I am always left thinking of at least some of the children I knew—the nine children whose dad, a fireman, was killed fighting a fire in 1959; or those other boys and girls, in the far-off time of the 1950s, waiting at the back door of the bakery, in winter, to get a piece of bread before they went to school.

Little Emma Cook boarding a ship with a second-hand doll to travel to New Brunswick in 1884 because someone somewhere thought that she was a problem that could be solved.

And I think of this at any dinner party when we talk of children.

It is also interesting to me to note the pretension of these views in the face of people who are unable to have children. People who cannot have children of their own are often looked upon with rather comic artificial sympathy.

Just as my mother was looked upon with sympathy—one that didn't even care to hide that it was false—because she had six children.

A professor once suggested kindly that my mother was a victim because she had a large family. He was shocked that I would for one moment hesitate to agree. It was not because of what he said that made me disagree but the inference he wished his remark to betray.

The inference was that my mother was never educated enough to make up her own mind, and couldn't, anyway, being as she was, a woman of the forties and fifties.

Which made her exactly what he considered her: being less than him.

And as an afterthought he told me in a whisper something he assumed I did not know: that *children suffered, too*.

His reasoning concurs: if Emma Cook, holding the second-hand doll in 1884, ready to get on a ship to Canada, had not been born, she would not have suffered. As if anyone could guarantee the degree of suffering of any human being, even himself.

To my professor, abortion was the new option, for Emma and her crew of unsavoury little rascals. To my professor, there was no real child in the procedure. But if that is the case, whose suffering was he stopping?

To me, nothing is more blinkered and more smugly self-assured than this view. They should not be born, but he was; they would have no chance at education, but he did. They would have no love of life, but his was immeasurable. They could not decide his fate, but he, with a sniff, could decide theirs.

I've also found that the stereotype that most conversations exhibit about the parents of large families is not better than the ones detergent commercials made of women in the fifties.

The bare bones of their argument has always struck me as this: that there should be a proper economic and intellectual table for being born that will forgo our need for charity, and moreover, there should be some way to implement this condition. Any father who argues with his child, or hustles him upstairs to make him take a bath and go to bed when he refuses at twelve years of age because he is rebelling, is not a father?

I make not one apology for it.

That is, the condition certain sociologists and approval-seeking writers want and need is a condition that would neglect a good many of the friends I value and probably myself. And most assuredly, many of the people who uniformly spout this argument. A few I know have never in their lives been able to show anything but conceited self interest.

It's similar to the principled upper classes long ago considering the poor as not human. Let's say, about the time William Blake was writing his *Songs of Innocence and of Experience*, or earlier still, when Jonathan Swift was writing *A Modest Proposal*.

I don't even think little Emma Cook would have given one second of her life for the casual opinion the professor had about her birth. Nor do I think that her suffering was not bountiful and filled with the same hope as his own children's. Maybe more so, across those storm-drenched seas.

What we really don't want is any more little Emma Cooks. In a way, it comes from a misguided noble sentiment: we do not wish humanity to suffer as we know she did.

If this is the sentiment, then the expedient measure is not to give her a chance at it. Cutting the head off a problem is one sure way to handle it. Setting her adrift on a ship to Canada is another.

The whole idea is that thinking this way is a psychic act of self-sacrifice on our part.

Rather like the portly overseer of some social program of the mid-1880s.

But one should never be the recipient of a benefit from one's own altruism, to the receiver of that altruism's debt.

I'm only saying this: It's fine altogether not to want something, or to never want it for others, either. But don't let us pretend it's because we care for it or them. Let not the childless writer virtue-signal in his books by filching an argument about children that he would never himself have to put to the test.

Let us not condemn so easily the young or poverty-stricken. Yes, some have made terrible mistakes as parents. So have the many sociologists and child activists who write so tenderly about it all. So have I. Just tell me to my face I wouldn't sacrifice my life for my children.

The real notes of hope come from the children themselves. Not those who garner them a problem. Come from Emma Cook, wherever that ship took her.

The doubters are ourselves.

Years and years ago, on the Miramichi, a tiny seven-year-old girl jumped off a dory into the bay to save her five-year-old brother. In spite of her courage she was unable to bring him to safety.

When a diver found the bodies some time later, they were sitting upright in the sand on the bottom, holding hands.

I've never yet heard dinner party concern about children that even comes close to such wisdom.

1991–2008

DRIVING AT NIGHT

FOR YEARS, I WORKED AT NIGHT. SOMETIMES IN THE WINTER I saw nothing more of the sun than a slight glow. I never minded too much. But wanting to get onto a day schedule caused all kinds of trouble. Generally no matter how much I tried, I slipped back into my nocturnal habits, boiled a pot of tea at midnight and went to work. For a number of years this caused a problem. If I had to travel from place to place, I couldn't start before the sun was down, because I wouldn't be awake enough to go. Never, when driving through to Ontario from the Miramichi, did I get onto the Plaster Rock Highway until after dark.

Sometimes in the winter, I travelled miles without meeting another car, and sometimes without seeing so much as a rabbit.

I don't think you see the world the same way anyway. Or the same things in the world. So often people are by themselves. And as we know from experience, there are few things in Canada that can kill, but the weather is one.

So you don't like to see people stranded.

There was a young man my wife and I picked up one night who hauled a switchblade on us, his arms tattooed with nunchucks, and his insistence that he had a black belt in karate.

My wife was driving, and as he sat behind me, holding the knife against the seat, he kept talking about going home to kick his brother in the head. The bumpy, battered road was empty for a long time.

He kept railing on, about some great things he had lost, someone who had deserted him.

Yes, I think all in all, tough boys are like drunkards. The less they say about it, the more you know they're the genuine article. After a while I told him he had to put his knife away. And he looked at it as if he was recognizing it for the first time, nodded and smiled. For the rest of the trip we talked about country and western music. Both of us were fans.

I don't remember where I was coming from when at two in the morning I went around a turn and in the dooryard of a small house saw a man, stark naked, waving an axe. As if he was limbering up for the local woodsman contest next day.

I saw him later on. In daylight he sat on the broken lawn chair fully dressed and stared benignly at the twisted road between Neguac and Burnt Church. And he's gone from us now. One day he just wasn't there anymore.

The house eventually got more and more solitary and deserted-looking, patched with dried-looking bushes and weeds, and after a time was torn down. I never knew who he was or learned his name. Nothing marks his spot now except part of a foundation: a grey, desolate chimney frame.

Being alone seems to be the thing about night travel. This is what I'm trying to say about it. Not only for myself but also for those I've met along the way.

Even when I tried to and planned to daylight-drive, I still was on the Plaster Rock at midnight.

It's a better road now than it once was, but still there are miles of what some would call "nothing." Trees and darkness. For a long time it wasn't paved.

One time in the late seventies I was travelling there:

I saw what I thought was a wounded deer.

It kept moving toward me out of the left darkness. I slowed down when it walked into the middle of the road and began to wave. He was covered in blood, wearing one shoe and holding the other in his hand, and his tie was twisted completely around. All the buttons of his shirt, except the one under his tie, were torn off, showing the friendly stretch marks of an enormous beer gut.

"How are you?" I asked.

"Not so bad—can you help me find my car?"

"Where did you last see it?"

"Somewhere in the ditch."

He should go to the hospital. But as you can guess, this wasn't his idea. His idea was that he would find his car and go home as quickly as he could. And being drunk, he was determined to find it before the cops did.

"It couldn't have snuck away too far," he said hopefully as to encourage my participation in the search.

But it wasn't anywhere he thought. That is, it wasn't in either ditch, and he had been wandering both sides of the road for a half hour looking for it.

His car was, we eventually saw, in the woods, about a hundred feet from the road, up against a spruce tree. He had no idea how it got there.

I told him to take the half-dozen broken and unbroken beer bottles and try to get rid of them. He thought about the best way to do this. And then he offered me one and we leaned against what was left of the hood.

"Weather's nice," he said.

"Pretty good," I said.

"On vacation, are ya?"

"I guess so," I said.

He hadn't remembered anything about going through the air, crossing the twenty-foot ditch and sailing into the woods. He hadn't remembered where he'd been, or where he was going. But what was worse for him was that he had lost the new teeth his family had gotten him for his birthday.

I suggested he must have lost them in the car, and looked about under the dash. A strange kind of invasion of privacy, I guess. But he kept searching the ground, swinging his shoe at the grass morosely, until another car pulled over.

I did happen to find his teeth near the brake pedal.

And we persuaded him to get in with those who had just stopped, to travel to Grand Falls, the closest hospital to us.

In the dark we were a few spots of light on the edge of nowhere. His hair greying, and his tie twisted completely about, as if he'd recently attempted to hang himself.

I never saw him again.

——

There was another night:

We were coming back from a wedding. It was after two in the morning. There was one other car in front of us. I told Peggy I couldn't chance to pass him because I couldn't tell when he might veer into the middle of the road.

He would do sixty and then slow down to twenty. He went around turns on the wrong side.

We were about thirty-five miles from Fredericton when he tried to go around a turn, crossed the centre line and went tumbling straight down a forty-foot embankment.

I went walking along the road, trying to spot him, and was joined in a minute by a man from New York.

Far down in the turn we could make out a feeble light and the sound of a woman—who I thought was speaking Spanish.

Then we saw them coming up the bank, and we scrambled down to meet them, the woman carrying a baby in her arms. They were from India, and the woman was dressed in traditional Hindu dress. The man was absolutely, painfully sober. A fact he wanted us to know. Though exhausted, he hadn't thought of pulling over.

At any rate the young fellow from New York went on his way, and we all walked to my car.

When they got into our back seat, I started to drive to the hospital in Oromocto (we were fifteen minutes from it).

"No, no," the gentleman said. "We must now go to the police station and make out the report."

The woman spoke to him for a second.

And he spoke angrily back: "But we must make out the report to the police, about my car."

Then they spoke for a few more moments in their language.

The woman told us she had been breastfeeding the baby, and it fell from her arms when the car went over the embankment.

"And now it doesn't want to wake up anymore," she said.

Everyone was silent. The night smelled sweet. It was in the middle of summer.

"Let me see it—I'll wake it," he said.

The man took the baby from her. And he began to flip him or her (I never found out which) into the air.

In my rear-view mirror, I saw the baby being tossed to the car ceiling, hover for a moment and come tumbling back down. Only to be flipped up again.

"I'll wake it—and then we'll go to the police and make out a decent report," the gentleman said.

We went to the hospital. The nurse got the baby to wake, and then a doctor took it. But I never heard from them again and am not sure what happened to their child.

Insanity can happen, drunk or sober, in the company of strangers.

And although I know the horrors of drunk driving, and have no sympathy for it, to tell the truth, between both men, I much preferred the drunk.

The last two cases involve holding hands:

The first one was on a train going through from Halifax to Newcastle some years ago. It was late at night.

The train was almost empty.

The moon shone down over the snow, and the sky looked like a grey chalkboard.

"Stop trying to hold my hand" I heard a woman say in back of me.

There had been a little fellow bothering her for some time, although no one knew.

First he walked by and sat with her. Then, when she moved her seat, he followed her—this was when they were behind me—and tried to hold her hand.

And after she told him that she didn't want to hold hands with him, he got up and walked by me.

He was about twenty-five, couldn't have been more than five feet two inches and wore lifts.

The train rocked its way through the woods, and everyone forgot about him.

Ten minutes later the car door banged open and he went flying past me with a conductor chasing him.

"That's him—that's him," a second woman yelled, following the conductor.

"That's him," the first woman said.

And he ran down to the end of the car, as fast as his legs would carry him, as another conductor cut him off. It seemed to me as if he was trapped. I didn't know how he'd get out of it. But never underestimate the value of panic.

Thwack.

He hit the conductor, who was trying to block his exit, square in the head, and the conductor staggered and went down.

And then he did what seemed to me to be absolutely unexpected. He jumped off the train.

We were out looking under the train for him at one in the morning. We did not find him.

"I hope he's not squished," one of the young women said, as the train started up again.

"He's not squished—you would have heard the squish," the other woman said.

A few of us looked out the train windows, into the grey silence.

The last case is similar to the others. Perhaps it is the archetypal case for those who drive at night.

It happened to a friend of mine. At three in the morning—coming back from somewhere. He left the road, and was thrown from his car. He lay in the ditch, his life going from him. No one about.

Until a young woman pulled over. They had never met before.

She told him she would have to go get him help, because it was in the middle of the night, and they were all alone.

"Oh no," he said, smiling at her for a second. "I'll be okay if you don't leave me. Just hold my hand, please hold my hand—and don't let go."

She took his hand and held on to it. Those were the last words he spoke.

I know these things aren't unusual or important whatsoever. But the memory of them has been with me for a long time. I have a kinder opinion now of the gentleman with the baby than I once had.

Being under stress he was only trying to do the right thing, not knowing his thinking was muddled. Perhaps new to our country, and conscious of bureaucratic reports, he was only frightened of being sent away.

Perhaps, too, it's summed up by the man I met on the Plaster Rock, the man with his tie twisted about his neck.

"Thank God you stopped," he said, smiling that wonderfully kind, self-deprecating smile so many New Brunswickers have. "Tonight, I'm on my own."

1994

LEE COULD NOT HAVE SPOKEN

THE GRAND OLD MAN OF THE CONFEDERACY, GENERAL LEE, spoke his last words, in delirium, in 1870: "Tell Hill he must come up" and "Strike the tent."

The first, an order to A. P. Hill, the red flannel-wearing general who had saved Lee's Army of Northern Virginia in 1862. The second was spoken to an unknown orderly to take Lee's tent down.

But now, after 120 years, they are being disputed. A College of Physicians insists that the damage Lee suffered in his stroke in the autumn of 1870 would not have permitted him to utter those words.

The trouble is, the pedantics are always right.

I have learned, however, that every time they stand on a point, they usually want to diminish someone else's reputation, sometimes that person's entire life. They never say this is their intent, but it is always evident in what they try to correct.

Lee could not have spoken.

In the fall of 1970, studying American history, I was told by an American professor that the Alamo had no heroes.

He hated the idea of war, and I can truly say I understand this. But because he did, he begrudged the very idea of heroics in war.

"There wasn't a hero there," he said to me. "They tried to surrender to General Santa Anna when the fort capitulated, before General Houston's troops arrived."

He seemed more than pleased with himself because of this opinion. One might ask: if he didn't believe in heroes, why was he so gleeful about what he obviously wanted me to consider a cowardly act?

At a party one evening in Fredericton someone quoted a beautifully succinct line from one of C. S. Lewis's essays on Christianity.

"How can you believe him?" someone said. "He was a cocaine addict." This one phrase made *him* seem all-knowing and C. S. Lewis a foolish old man indeed.

Another time, someone got angry and self-righteous because they heard Van Gogh had only cut off his earlobe, and not the whole ear. It seemed that this action was not worth Van Gogh's life's work and so made him something of a fraud. And this same person had heard that Churchill had decided not to warn Coventry it was going to be bombed, in order to prevent the Germans from discovering that the Brits had deciphered their code. This made him realize, he said, that Churchill was "no better than Hitler." And felt appalled. Which is what he said:

"I feel appalled."

The trouble is most of the rest of us tried to apologize to him. We were sorry Churchill did this, and could he forgive us for not being as appalled as he was.

"No—I'm just appalled."

There are always ways in which being stingily correct will reduce everyone else to our level.

We must get a great deal of pleasure out of it.

A woman I know sat in a poet's den one day and picked out the three or four spelling mistakes in his book of poems. She said nothing else about the book.

Of course it reduced everything to where she sat. She was only being helpful. Not capable of writing a book of verse herself, she was genuinely interested in only what was wrong with his.

"Oh—here's a mistake" were her first words after she had picked up the book.

"How right you are," the poet said, looking at it.

And she smiled around at us all.

The poet smiled, too.

When I knew this woman, she continually used the method of convenient empathy. Faint praise not to damn but to democratize. This is the same lady who, every time you told her of someone being up for an award, said, almost in tears, "Oh, I'm so afraid they'll lose." Until you realized that she was praying that no one ever win anything—but her.

These peculiar people come in all shapes and sizes, all races and religious affiliations. Their thoughts are programmed by CBC Radio talk and Oprah Winfrey.

You meet them at any party you go to, all summer barbecues and any skating rink, too, and it is reputation they are after. They are the highly educated, unthinking, literal minded. They always hold others accountable for the ability to think for themselves.

Even in this essay, to say that you admire General Lee is, for some of them, to be in favour of antebellum slavery. You will be accused of racism for saying that the rebels fought well, with little to fight with.

(That is like saying that Churchill, who admired Rommel, was in favour of Hitler; or that thousands of troops, and generals who fought against Lee and called him an honourable man, were on his side. In fact, the first thing soldiers of the Army of the Potomac would say about a new commander was "He might be good, but he ain't yet fought Bobby Lee.")

You never win. As Tolstoy comments, the stupid always have the initial argument. Yet somehow God gives us grace. The pedantic always fail. That's the thing. Wait long enough.

Those who ridiculed F. Scott Fitzgerald in those lonely thirties killed him but never destroyed him, and don't matter a damn now. Or Dostoevsky, him.

Or General Grant's friends, who called him "a drunk" behind his back and went whining to Lincoln about him, never mattered much once Richmond fell.

But of course, beware. These people just change tack and keep going.

Not only do some of them change horses in midstream, they put on a different bridle and bit and change the stream itself.

Some of them change opinion about people with the same grace as changing underwear.

"He couldn't have done that" or "She's not as good as you think" is forever on their lips, as a way to explain you to me, and to shore themselves up for tomorrow.

They never meet you on even ground, these ladies and gentlemen. They are forever at your throat, or at your feet. They are on every Passion window in every church. But it is never themselves being nailed to the cross.

1990–2009

THE TURTLE, THE HANDBOOK,
THE DARK NIGHT AIR

I WAS WALKING ALONG A SPANISH BEACH WITH MY SON. IT WAS December and the clouds had formed darkish pink spirals above us, far away and beautifully made. Above those clouds the sky was still and frigid. The air was sharp, and a man had lit a fire under a palm tree, burning off garbage to keep warm. The gardens were still, the lights from the rows of white villas shone in a peculiar winter way, while whole blocks of *apartamentos* were boarded shut. Waiting for the German, Swiss and British clientele to arrive in April.

Night was coming and we were searching the beach for bamboo sticks to take back to our villa. Some we would use to start the fire—others, the best ones, we would use to play our game of hockey. The best ones were sturdy, with knots at the bottom, hooked out like the blade of a hockey stick.

My son wore his Montreal Canadiens sweater, and sweatpants and sneakers, running in and out of the water, not at all worried about getting wet. He was four years old. Far off in the Mediterranean the black outline of the island of Ibiza made me remember other trips here, while against the mountains and wintry haze to our north was the illumination from the far-off city of Valencia.

I remembered Ibiza because I had visited that island twenty-five years before with my brother. At that time we had travelled all along this coast by ship, living for two weeks in a Spanish Civil War bunker on the Canary Islands, off the coast of Africa. On the way back our tramp steamer ran into foul weather, a hurricane, which knocked all the passengers out of commission.

There were many African students going up to study in Spain or France in March of 1971. Everyone except myself and a London boy named Dennis Mahoney took seasick. For four days and nights the waves came up over the ship, the ship moaned and tossed, and Dennis and I made our way up to the galley to eat our meals—two people at a table set for forty.

I remembered this while on the beach with my son, and thought that time was obligated to pass—just as our parents told us it would—too fast. I will never see Dennis again, or his friend John Cruise, who did two tours in Northern Ireland for the British Army. At night he would sit up, still asleep, and swish his Bowie knife in the air above our heads.

"They aren't coming," Dennis would whisper. "John—John— they aren't coming."

He had bad dreams.

We go along the beach and my son is a master at finding sticks. The sand is cold and the beach is built up with bars and restaurants specializing in local seafood dishes. Paella during the afternoon. Sometimes it is hard to get paella after a certain hour of the day, and I have always considered it an evening meal.

There is a sense you have here of restaurants and bars and cafés dominating the world. After a month in Spain the idea of being a waiter strikes my son as being the best job in the world.

We have collected our sticks. The beach seems deserted, far as the eye can see. It is almost night. Yet I see something in the waves. A body of some sort. I turn and walk toward it. And then step out into the cold December water, where I detect its outline.

A woman begins to talk very quickly in Spanish to me, and then, when her eyes meet mine, she recognizes me as not one of hers. She smiles.

She is struggling in waist-high water with a giant dead turtle that has floundered in front of her small bar. And at first I think that the young woman—whose blouse and jeans are now soaking wet— wants to put the turtle farther into the sea. But then with some hand direction and broken English and Spanish, I realize she wants to haul it up on the beach, where my son is watching, and where the tractor will come and clear it away on Tuesday. But she can't make any headway with it alone.

I grab one of the turtle's back flippers and we haul it in. It is a large, old turtle. At one certain place something on its flippers or broken shell is rough enough to cut open my left hand—though not my right one. My left hand is my "bad" hand, as my son named it, and although my right arm is quite strong, I have a hard time picking up a cup of coffee with my left. Not that it is so weak—it is not. I just have no coordination or any real control over its movement.

The secret is my left leg, too, is "bad," and has almost gotten me killed half a dozen times or more. Usually from falling. From tripping on anything. From tumbling over a cliff when I was a child. Or from falling under trains when I jumped them as a kid. From falling off logs while fishing, to missing ice floes when I jumped them in the spring breakups long ago. And once slipping out from under me, when I was wearing chest waders, alone in the middle of the Northwest Miramichi. I went floating and flailing about, upside down for a while.

I think of these things as we haul the turtle to shore. I don't know how it died, or what has ripped open its shell: age, disease, a dogfish or shark.

My son and I walk farther up the beach under those golden-tinged clouds spiralling above our heads.

"¡Gracias!" the young woman shouts after us, wiping her brow, in the final dusk of the Spanish evening. "¡Muchas gracias!"

"De nada, señorita—de nada."

In the night air outside my villa, drinking a Bitter Kas, I wash and wrap my bleeding hand, while my son watches me with the hope that I will wrap and bandage his hand, as well. And so of course I do, and he runs back and forth with his left hand bandaged just like mine. In the winter in Canada when I wrap my left hand because of arthritis, he does the same thing. I, too, have often, like a lost child, imitated friends and loved ones I admired. At least for a little while. As long as I thought they admired me.

It has always caused me problems—this hand—my left side. I should have come to terms with it long ago, because a wooden leg is an excuse for nothing, Thomas Wolfe said. And I firmly believe that he is right. But it wasn't him as much as me who would know.

Of course, in most ways I have come to terms with it, as with everything else, the injury I suffered when my mother fell off a porch when she was seven months pregnant, landing on her stomach and causing me to be born that night. I have made fun of it a lot more than others; I scorn it every day. Yet I can't ignore it.

One photographer put it this way: "Most people worry about a traumatic experience interrupting their lives, but freaks have suffered their trauma at birth." Something at least a little like that.

I have never been frightened of injury or physical violence, and certainly not death, so much as ridicule because of it.

Anyway, it is not so readily noticeable to those who don't know me. Yet everything I have done has been done with my right side, aware of my left side being limited, non-existent.

Because of this I have squared myself to the world with one side, doing things I might not have done or not doing things I should have. At least, I think this is the reason. Other factors are involved.

I have struggled across rapids, canoed rivers and been stranded in the middle of the Miramichi Bay at midnight, drifting slowly out to sea, and have always been secretly afraid of water.

There are always other factors.

The old turtle reminds me of my youth, and remembering some bigger boys who teased a poor old turtle with a hole through its shell, chained to the backyard fence. There were yellow leaves on the ground, and it crawled to the corner of the yard to hide.

Later when I was older, some boys were tormenting a porcupine, and I came along with my shotgun and killed it. I don't know if I killed the right animal, but something had to be done.

There is music. It goes on and on. But like all music it only lasts so long, and later, much later, you will hear the shutters being drawn, the sound of laughter in the dark night air like boys and girls on the Miramichi.

A man I know walked into a party on the Miramichi one time and was hit in the face with a shovel. It was a case of mistaken identity.

One night when I was nineteen and in the wrong town, I was mistaken for someone else, and ended up fighting two men. I was arrested by the brother of one of these men and thrown into a cop car. The brother was arrested with me, or for appearance' sake brought to the police station and then let go.

He would hit me, swinging cross the chest of his brother, sitting between us, and each time I went to hit him back, his brother, the police officer, would whack me with his billy club across the knees. It became a game of paddywhack. With me being whacked. I knew if I could hit him with my right hand, he would feel it, but they had cuffed my right hand to his left, around the back of the seat, and I only had my left to swing with.

I have been often asked why I became a writer. I had to. I had no choice. There was nothing else I could do. I had a need to write about and remember, and give some voice to my terrible youth.

In the air, the Spanish air, I think of the turtle. I think of the moose chased across ice by dogs years before. Another moose I shot and had to climb inside to gut.

The Miramichi and Spain are not such awkward places to correlate the connection between act and compassion, or act and violence.

There is a great swell out in the sea. I hear it crashing away against the painted slips, the lawn chairs turned over and filled with fallen leaves.

I often think of the young man herring-fishing in our bay a number of years ago. A storm came up and he couldn't make it back to the wharf. His last words to shore, out into the cold, foul dark, were: "Can't talk no more boys—I'm goin' down."

In some ways I modelled my favourite character, Ivan Basterache, from *Evening Snow Will Bring Such Peace*, on him.

People live through terrible experiences and experience full lives and never recognize anything.

Others see while throwing down pulp from a truck stuck on the bridge over Little River, helping a truck driver who's had a heart attack and his frightened ten-year-old son, everything that ever needs to matter about the world. It is never the action, but why the action, that must be understood by us all.

It is cold here in December. My child freezes under his blankets, and we have to keep a heater going. However, in the day, by noon, the sun warms us enough that we can walk about in a T-shirt.

In local and regional literary circles I became well known by the time I was twenty-two. As time goes along I see it much clearer than I once did, realize I was cared for by some but resented by others. The problem was that for a time I was too young to know, because I was resented or envied by many I truly admired.

One idea my critics used was that I wrote bad things about my river and my people. No other writer in the Maritimes that I can think of has ever suffered this maligning of intent more than I.

Far over my head the December sky, and palm trees glisten in the lights from the bar up the street. My son is in bed and I've come to Spain to write a novel, hoping as with every novel I write that this novel will be my last—and then knowing that as long as I live it cannot be.

In the literary world I once knew, compassion and radical thought played out on the surface, like coins off the skirts and tweeds of women and men. Very few, however, jumped trains. They promoted ideas of motherly non-violent compassion without ever coming close to a reason it was needed. They might not jump trains, ice floes, spear fish or kill or injure anything in the world, some of them believed. Most of them had never had a punch to the head as hard as I had when my mother fell at seven months.

But it is a strange thing about the lesson of the turtle this black night in Spain, and how it painfully cut open my hand. It is this: That never does a second pass when you are ever certain of the comfort of a second ago. And that no matter who you are, nothing, not even the intellectual comfort and safety of a group, will last forever.

My son knows the problem. Once when I helped him through the waves on the beach in Australia he winced:

"Dad," he said, "you got me with your badder hand."

I have little control over how much force I am using when I hold something with it. That is why my hand is often cut. I have cut it on windows and door handles, chunks of ice.

I have bruised my son half a dozen times by accident, and have been brought to tears seeing the black bruises that he does not complain about, that my fingers have left on his arm.

I share this affliction with others.

A sailor I know fell from the top of the Angus L. Macdonald Bridge, in Halifax. When he hit the water, it sounded like a .303, and he now has no use of his left arm. He, too, wraps it in the winter, sometimes heats it with a small butane lighter and burns himself.

When once I asked him about this, about my left hand aching now all winter long, he nodded:

"Ache—oh yeah—it'll always ache—no problem there."

And he smiled his toothless smile.

He tries to drink it, and other things, away. For seventeen years, so did I.

———

In so many books published it is all a package of social concern and neighbourly wisdom now, like crystals of instant soup. The trick is to pretend it's your wisdom as you step up to the podium to read. If you do this well enough, you'll win the Pulitzer Prize. Carry this handbook guide written out for you, and don't misplace it with all the others in the crowded room:

A single mother suffers.
Men do not understand women.
A drunken father is brutal.
Fights in police cars are bad.
Ignorance and violence are always male.
Racists are always white.
The age of intellectual comfort has come.

You may believe it's all true, though you might not know any of it well, or why it is. But there is a checklist in the handbook for all of these things now. It has all been prepared for you. Others, too, have had the same list prepared for them.

Like instant coffee in a Styrofoam cup, it's always all there, ready to mix up. It takes a lot of encouragement to swallow. But the payoff means you belong to the inner circle, the compassionate ones of gentle autumn book launchings and luncheons with privileged ladies who are bound to agree with you on what true suffering means.

Suffering. That is of course the word, isn't it? I began to write at the very moment the age turned toward this complete handbook of instant knowledge and compassion about suffering. There was always a way to buy the handbook. The checklist was always there. It was to deny that you were ever the one to humiliate or inflict pain and by this admission take yourself to task. *Suffering* was always caused by others, and you knew whom those others were. Nothing was better than to single them out, and exonerate oneself.

Violence was always unthinkable in that certain little group I once knew. Social concern replaced charity. Today so much writing has become indifferent to suffering in any real way because it deals with all suffering, as with everything, in a way that accommodates the handbook. I've seen the handbook. You notice it in how certain people react over anything that cannot be controlled. You notice it more in how they instantly freeze out anyone who has really suffered.

It goes a long way to relieve much of the responsibility of introspection.

Most of them will never understand the tragedy they have partaken in.

"I will never write about pain that isn't mine," Alden Nowlan once said.

The truth is, you can't. Eighty percent of the books published today prove this as an incalculable truth.

I think of this now in Spain. That there was always an idea inherent with certain people I knew from that side of my life, that they are not the ones to be able to hurt anything. That they were in positions of a certain favour. That even angels would have their wings bloodied before they would bloody their hands. That they could not stomach to maim or hurt. A posture finally for all the others with the same handbook, the same set of rules.

Still, I realize now that literature through the ages does not very often favour those who have the handbook, though they hold on to it like a treasure. But literature favours in the end Emily Brontë's torch. The torch illuminates the one who remains steadfast in searching the foul night, either in laughter or in tears—searching, and knowing what it is they are searching for. That's the key.

All around, everywhere there will be cold and darkness. I'll say this: there is no shame to recognize it as such. The world is and must be and always has been a brutal, mad and godless place filled with priceless moments of hilarity, sacrifice and love. That is what the torch is for. That's the reason for it. To search this out. There is no shame to carry it. Someone will always have to. It's just that you've got to be sure you know *why* it has to be carried the way it is.

The best part, not the worst, remains with the man and woman who finally understand this, whether they write comedy or tragedy.

The best part after all the hoopla is over, and the age does pass (for the age will pass), will not belong to those I have known driven by as frantic an urge to conform as I've ever seen. Who hold up their handbooks like passports in a crowded queue.

Finally someday, the best part will belong as it always has, with the greater kindness and virtue, and love for life of an Ivan Basterache, a Cathy McDurmot, a Jerry Bines.

The best part belongs, no matter how big or little, brave or frightened we all can be, the best part belongs to those who know that there is a reason to scorn the handbook, a reason to enter the sea, to cut open a hand or to hit back in defiance at the darkness that has reduced or tormented the neglected ones, be they rich or poor, good or bad.

They are still the ones who rely upon us to acknowledge them. The turtle, the porcupine, the cripple thrown in jail. The tragedy is leaving them out by conventionalizing how they suffer; maligning those who know what their suffering really means; refusing to let go of the handbook that lies both about you and them. Telling untruth for the hope of immediate applause.

This is what the dark night tells us, as pitched and worrisome as it is. It is after all the only thing writers like Shakespeare, Dostoyevsky or Emily Brontë would have us give a piss for.

On that, boys and girls, I will stake my life.

1996–2014

AN ANECDOTE

IT WAS A VERY WARM SPRING NIGHT IN PARIS, AND I WAS celebrating having a book published there. So I went with my French publisher to have supper at a restaurant near the Louvre. My host was not an expansive person. He was rather retentive, attentive, quiet. In fact I discovered over the two days with him that he bought his paper in Indonesia because it was cheaper, and therefore this would hold the printing of books, such as my book, up.

So he was prudent. He was part of society seen in many artistic circles one would call more "diligent" than "inventive." A person who, if he wrote lines of poetry, would struggle over the exact word rather than ever have that word come naturally. You find this among poets who have given their lives to academia, and believe in academia even when academia betrays them for the twentieth time.

I suppose I make too much over searching for the right word. There is not a thing wrong with that, except we have seen many of those who have studied much and long in creative writing courses, some of them having pared poems down until there is no poem left.

Diligent, yes, but there is a deficiency to it all, an absence of some sort, isn't there? In fact the right word is so often not found. Or at least, the feeling behind it is absent.

How must we feel about a writer who gets good notices for a poem that has been fed through a group conscience? Well, let us feel about him the same way we would about a person who shouts *shame* when they are taught to or *yea* when they are told to, and are silent or confused over any idea that does not fit the affiliated symposiums. I do not know if this was entirely the prerogative of my French publisher, but I do know this: he felt privileged enough about his position to make statements and decisions concerning me.

The dinner was pleasant enough. The Louvre was bathed in light; our restaurant was in a glass corridor that ran along the side of the courtyard. There was no sound of traffic, and Paris overall is a wondrous city at night. Actually, a wondrous city at any time. One walks about during the day and comes across a statue to Montaigne, a statue to Voltaire. The tomb of Napoleon, and the Cathedral of Notre-Dame, where I saw what was thought to be the armour of one of my favourite people from history, Joan of Arc. You marvel at the architecture, the brilliant symmetry of the buildings, the bridges crossing the Seine.

One knows they are walking the streets Joan of Arc and François Villon did walk, and Van Gogh, and Picasso, Fitzgerald, James Joyce and Hemingway, too.

Then you think: What if Hitler in his worming madness had succeeded in burning it? Or in lassoing those masterpieces from the Louvre that Göring salivated over? How despicable all of this would have been to the world. One sometimes thinks this when they are sitting looking at Vermeer. At any rate I did think this later that night and for many a night after.

It was soon to be the sixtieth anniversary of D-Day. I did not mention this. I had no reason to mention it. But I had relatives and the fathers of friends of mine shot up on that day. I was good friends of a person who had lost his legs. My wife's uncle was shot carrying a radio through a town a mile or so from the beach. He lived and his grandson visited the spot where he had been shot, met an old man who was a young man then, who for years thought the Canadian soldier had died until he met his grandson.

My father went through the Blitz. His best friend was shot down in his Spitfire. Canadian boys died heroically on the beaches of Dieppe. Canadian women parachuted behind enemy lines and were captured, tortured for days, raped and executed. Canadian nurses held their positions under fire. The Canadians fought because it was morally right in a world gone mad. There was no other choice. Surrender wasn't an option, not even for the French who surrendered. I did not mention it.

My publisher had chicken and cauliflower. His partner had white wine and venison. I opted for chicken and potatoes and a black coffee. We were all dressed casually but well. I have a picture taken at that time by a French photographer. I was still youthful. I suppose I still believed in my career.

The meal was almost over—we had talked of books, we spoke of Alistair MacLeod, and Coetzee, and John Ralston Saul. We spoke about John Updike and how awful were our Canadian winters. We spoke about European soccer and the European Union. We spoke about liberal politics and the world's unity. Yes, it was my meal with my French publisher, so all the topics were about the same as with any of my other publishers. The world of literary men and women had come to a consensus of right and wrong, which I never seemed to be a part of. I said nothing.

I was actually thinking of telling them about two men I knew who stopped in the middle of D-Day's horror and violence to help deliver a baby because a young Frenchwoman in a house near the fighting had gone into premature labour.

I was just about to mention this, when my publisher said, "Oh, I received a letter from the Canadian embassy for you."

"Oh?" I said.

"Yes—I answered for you," he said.

"Oh? You did?"

"Of course. *Oui*. There was no reason for you to answer it." He poured himself a glass of wine and smiled.

"Well, yes, but what was the letter about?"

"Well, it is about their awful celebration," he said.

"I see—what awful celebration is that?"

"You know—D-Day—they invited you to attend that celebration next month. But I simply said, 'Anyone who writes as sensitively as Mr. Richards would never want to attend anything that glorifies war.'"

He smiled at me, reached over and squeezed my hand. His partner smiled. They shook their heads at the inanity of the invitation. Yes, what a fiasco that must have been. War, and how right they were to bravely denounce it all.

His partner poured herself another glass of wine, as well. Sometimes these subjects are so trying it is very difficult to speak of them sober. I stared at them both a long moment in silence. I could not speak to it. I had suddenly lost my voice and my appetite for the meal. I seemed to have lost a lot more by exclusion from a ceremony I would have been honoured and humbled to attend. But I would not tell them that—you see neither of them deserved to hear it.

It is too bad they weren't there at that time—you know, on D-Day to protest war the way they so heroically did now.

My anecdote about bravery and goodness, and aiding in a young Frenchwoman giving birth on June 6, 1944, I left unsaid.

2016

DRIVE-IN THEATRE

MY FATHER BOUGHT A DRIVE-IN IN 1958, AND RAN IT UNTIL IT
went down in the sun sometime in 1983. From there we showed
movies that were second or third run. The drive-in sat on a few acres
of land strewn with gravel, the canteen and projection booth sitting out in the middle, white and desolate as an adobe, and during
the afternoon the whole place had the strange effect of otherworld-
liness, of one being on an alien world, some strange planet at the
end of the solar system, somewhere that was shown on the screen
in 1959. The white speaker poles stretched back to the end of the lot,
like strange, desperate soldiers; the grand, large plywood screen sat
like a reflector, reflecting what we wanted or at least waited to see.
And in the day it was so deathly still, and hot, with the sun's glare on
the flat earth; the on-again off-again clicking of grasshoppers made
it even quieter. It was as if we were part of a movie somewhere, on
someone else's screen, and someone imitating James Dean would
come driving up in his Lil Bastard. The grasshoppers would jump
out of my way as I walked across the crunching gravel and during

the daylight showed that another world was there, just beneath our feet, a world of grasshoppers, and small hills where ants still planned and conducted their lives, held meetings, went on trips. Now and again the summer wind blew the trees in the distance, or scattered the little mounds of dust, like the sad memory of watching Natalie Wood walk away from some young lover, of Joanne Woodward in *No Down Payment* laughing because her life is in ruins.

It was all my father ever knew, the business, the hall—this is what we called the two theatres in town, that our family owned, *the hall*. We were the only people in town who did not call our business by the names they were known. Everyone else might say, "I am going to the theatre" or "I am going to a movie." Or "I'm going to the Opera House" or "I am going to the Uptown."

I would ask my mom, "Where is Dad?"

"Down at the hall."

That is because when our family started the business of glitz and glamour attracting the good townsfolk of Newcastle, to what many back then would call "sin," my grandparents played in a hall. This was back in 1911, after my grandfather arrived on the Miramichi from London, England, at the start of his proposed North American piano tour. He planned on going from Halifax to Vancouver and then crossing into the States, and travelling back from Seattle to New York, where by then he was hoping to be famous. Well, it didn't quite work out that way. He got to Newcastle, New Brunswick, without a violin accompanist, and had to advertise for one in the local paper. A young lady of eighteen by the name of Janie McGowan auditioned. He asked her if she could read music; she said no, that she could not, but that she could play anything he could. And their partnership was cemented. They played together at the old town hall, and then opened a theatre together, and our livelihood was born. It was born of that union. We were the first independent theatre in the Maritimes, and probably the last. Out of that was born all our blessings and our agony, our nights of playing for the silent films of D. W. Griffith, and Charlie Chaplin, Buster Keaton and Fatty Arbuckle, playing talking movies, and owning two theatres, closing one down in the age of television, then opening the drive-in and playing second and third runs, dusk till dawn, our midnight specials. Our nights of praying in the church, of my sister being confronted about sin at the convent for running movies in the fifties—with a stern-looking, uncharitable matron of the cloth looking straight ahead as she spoke, enough not to fill us with dread, but to tell us we, like Gypsies, were to many always part of the outcast lot, the ones who did the show, not the ones who snuck into it. It is strange to think, but we were always in some way an outcast lot. That is why when I gave all else up to be a writer, the last thing that bothered me was that people would consider me different. I had been really since I was born. Starving was just an added obstacle.

In the early years there were the internecine wars with other families who tried to take over our business, in the 1920s after my grandfather died. My grandmother trying to keep her head above water after they tried to at first buy her out, then foreclose on her mortgage with a corrupt and in-debt manager of the Royal Bank, and then finally bomb her out. All of this came in the twenties when my father was a boy; all of this left him with a certain devotedness to his mother, to the business, and a kind of ambivalence toward others. Years later, as I sat in the tavern, an older gentleman came in and bought me a beer, thinking I was Janie McGowan's son. I told him I was her grandson. He was surprised that so much time had elapsed. When he left me, a friend of mine told me that he was one of the, at the time, young men who was hired to blow my grandmother's business sky-high. He was, I think, saying he was sorry with that beer. At any rate I hold nothing against him.

My father was not like other fathers or other men. Not in our town he wasn't. He wasn't a professional, so had no contact with those who were; he was not a union boy and had no contact there, either. He was not in retail or had a clothing store—there were plenty of those. He had a theatre; it was a sacred duty to him, to do what his mother needed him to do. That is, in a certain way he had no other life—and we were left to decide who we were. My family is a strange combination of children who grew up really without a father because he had almost no time for us. Nor was he distinctive of any class. So we grew to adulthood, my brothers and sisters, where some of us were middle class and some were working class. That is, whom we strongly identified with was very much different among children born a year or two apart to the same mother and father.

Back to the drive-in—here where I walked, cleaning the lot on those summer days, alone, using a stick with a nail as a spear, picking up paper cups and empty containers, used prophylactics, as the wind blew dust up in little squalls—saddened by the emptiness of it all—that was where my father's soul was—where it had to be. It was up there on the desperately blank plywood screen—that looked fifty or sixty feet high—where heads would appear at night as big as tractors, and cars in our lot, filled with moms and dads and squabbling kids, would be watching from far below.

My father's soul could and would be nowhere else. His family had the business in town and he borrowed the money—so much money then for him he showed my brother and I the cheque in some astonishment, and bought one more outlet to entertain the public. But it was a public he had not that much to do with.

I often watched him with other men, hoping that he had a connection with them—with any of them, really; with anyone at all, really—and he never quite did. The only things he had a connection with were in celluloid, up there, in the night. That's where he belonged, from the time he was born. In the end I don't think he really belonged anywhere else.

Everything he did he had to do himself, learn by himself and measure for himself. There was no one to help him. His father was a diabetic patient of Banting and Best, but died in treatment in Montreal in 1923. There is a rather short but poignant letter I have from the doctor there—given to me by my cousin Catherine, a notice of his death written to my grandmother. That is all I have of my grandfather, and what my father had of his. He left behind a wife and three children, and a small business in a nondescript part of the world, a world away from the world he must have envisioned for himself when he left England over a decade before. My father walking the drive-in yard in 1961 was the benefactor and also the victim of that world, bringing what must have seemed like exotic places and climes to our hometown. That and the fact that he reminded his Irish stepfather of the English bloke Janie McGowan had first married were some of the reasons for the hundred beatings he took.

But he never spoke of that once to me; or to anyone, really. But it did make him more devoted to his mother, and to the business that he came back to help run after the Second World War. That is when his narcolepsy became noticeable. His sleeping sickness. Perhaps it was his escape. But he was grounded from flying a Spitfire and remained on duty in London.

He was a big man with a barrel chest, and large hands. He could have been a stagecoach driver like his own grandfather, or a woodsman like some of his uncles. He could have worked the docks, but all of that had been in a way denied him. It is strange to say that kind of work was denied him, when the work in a business was granted. But in a way that is how I feel when I think of him. Friendships were denied, as well. His must have been a lonely adolescence. When we were children and played hockey—or when my older brother who had some real talent did—I would see him at the games, cheering, usually alone. Sometimes with another man his age, who would look upon him as a curiosity. Someone who may have grown up beside him but had formed no meaningful relationship with him.

But he had a relationship with the movies. He explained to me once, and it took him a good twenty minutes, how they were now making the dinosaur monsters better—oh yes, long, long before *Jurassic Park*. They were able to make them look more alive. He was pleased with that, and pleased when later after I saw the movie he touted, I told him I believed he was correct.

"Yes—they swing their tails better now—and their eyes move so you almost believe they are looking at you," he said. It was almost as if he was going to say, "What will they think of next?"

Of course he was always comfortable with children, because hundreds surrounded him every week at movies and matinees. Sach and the Bowery Boys; the Little Rascals; Abbott and Costello. He ran those on long-ago Saturday afternoons at our theatre downtown. There might be snow and wind outside, but in the darkness of that hall, children could imagine the world away on city streets, see New York and London, fly to the jungles of Africa. The children cheered and yelled, and traded comic books before the lights went down. Almost every Saturday someone lost someone. Or something.

"My sister lost her mitten—it's red."

"Have you seen my brother—he has freckles."

"I lost my money for my bag of chips—and now I can't get a bag of chips."

The child would get a bag of chips.

He was always patient with them; his relationship with children came because in some way—in some deep, hopeful way—I believe that is where he could hide. He could hide in the children's movies that he ran on a Saturday afternoon, and be ten or twelve years old all over again. He could hide there and not be beaten—or alone, because so many children gathered around him now, like friends he never had when a boy.

He never fit into the adult world he was forced to live in. Oh, he pretended he did, and people very well might have thought so, but we his own children knew better.

He had never been allowed to. It is strange, but sometimes I think there might have been one movie he was looking for—the proverbial movie he could hide in, as well.

From thirteen to sixteen I worked at the drive-in in the summer months, got my paycheque out of petty cash—sometimes a nice twenty-dollar bill along with a five and a two. I would hand french fries out, or hand out speakers down at the ticket shed—that is, when we stopped having speakers attached to the poles and had them stored in boxes. The workers came and went, the cooks, the canteen staff, the projectionists, all of them or many of them living off petty cash, as well, as close to Hollywood and fame as any of us would ever get, I suppose.

His favourite actress was Irene Dunne. And Bette Davis. He loved Alan Ladd in *Shane* and Gary Cooper in *High Noon*. He ran *Moby Dick* again, and *Gone with the Wind*. The only problem with *Gone with the Wind* was just after Butterfly McQueen said, "Oh, Miss Scarlett, I don't know nothin' 'bout birthin' no babies," the screen went dead. Our projectionist tried to find the last reel, but it wasn't there, and finally my father told the patrons to come back tomorrow night at the same time; the last reel would be found, and they could listen to Clark say to Scarlett, "Frankly, my dear, I don't give a damn."

And before they left, he would give anyone who wanted, a free french fry and a Coke.

When people showed their displeasure, they lay on their horns, and flashed their lights. Some, when the speakers were still attached to the poles, would drive away and tear the speakers off.

I am not exactly sure if we ever got the last reel of *Gone with the Wind* that time around. But slowly my father's business was up against it—slowly the engine of progress worked against him, against open-air theatres in general—slowly the age of theatres became streamlined and monopolies began to take control. Just as when my grandmother a generation before had to face her adversaries and borrow money against her business from a lumber baron so she would not be forsaken, and travel to Montreal to get the monopoly on the talkies, now others were coming along. Famous Players asked to buy my father out and he said no. But you see, a movie theatre exists of first runs. You have to run a movie before your competition if you want to stay in business. So we closed the Opera House because of television, and then little by little the Uptown lost its place among the corporations, and he started to lose his first runs. The distributors for Fox and Paramount, and MGM made contracts with the Famous Players theatre across the river, and he was left with United Artists. He struggled on. He would not give up or in. He was protecting his mother's legacy and that of his father, who he remembered only slightly as a shadow of a man in bed.

One night he took a shotgun and went across to the drive-in to sit in the canteen to stop the break-ins into our stock room that the police didn't seem able to solve. He was, as always, alone—and of course the ragamuffins who worked for him had relayed the message to those who stole from him that he was sitting there with a shotgun. So that night no bandits came.

He had not caught on to what I knew from the time of ten: the idea of where loyalty laid.

One of the real reasons he lost his first runs at the theatre is that he could not afford them. In a small town like ours you might get away with showing a first run for five days—but to be told you had to run it longer or you could not get it—or if you did get it for five days like you asked, you would have to pay the company 60 percent—meant that your profit margin was so slim it wasn't worth it. But if you didn't take it, then you would not be considered an outlet for their product. That is, they would take other movies from you. This was the debacle my father began to face when he became a sole independent. They wanted him gone, in one way or the other. And he, as always, was alone.

Little by little then, little by little, flesh took over the screen. Perhaps he didn't even notice. The Hammer films of the fifties and sixties, where the tops of the ladies came off during an earthquake or being chased by a monster; to the *Story of O* and other semi-erotic masterpieces of the late sixties and early seventies, like *Emmanuelle* or the more elaborately and openly sexual *99 Women*. In these movies, the women were submissive and open to all suggestion, from titillation to anal sex to whippings. If they were not open, they were as repressed as nuns. But many of these movies took place in convents, so the nun's erotic predilections could be exposed, as well. The men were supposedly all-knowing, sexually urbane, often middle aged and wearing something like corsets to hide their stomachs, where learning to have intercourse in a hundred different positions was the high point of their civilized behaviour, and showed that all was and were equal. All other human emotion was absent except sexual mimicry. But you see, it was all still verboten. That was the secret of it—exciting because it was all still taboo. The sex comedies were always in my mind the most mindless—showing that sex was profane, naughty and a sin, while pretending it was all for a good laugh and bashing the ministers of the church and the church ladies who in secret performed oral sex on young seminarians. (*ha ha ho*)

The drive-in movie theatres were always open to those movies, showed them for one reason: to have cars by the poles. I am not sure I can detail how it came about—except to say a new independent strain of movie was happening, with many divergent asides, believing it was an exercise in expression and sexual liberation. This looking back was as nonsensical as some of the queries of the new #MeToo movement today, the new safe-space attitude of young women and men—but it all comes from the same place if you look closely enough at it. The regimental idea of who we are supposed to be forced upon us by popular culture that ends in a kind of hysteria, and will not stop until there is a sudden shift of focus. Then it will seem as pallid as most other things, and be exposed for what it is.

Seeing these movies again, on the internet, is to realize how pallid and infantile most were—and how easy the dark web can transport you from those movies into the darker regions of our psyche within a minute—and how essentially all these movies can be brought into any home at any second of the day. There is nothing at all upsetting about most of it, excepting when they insist it frees one. For the price is always there, to be paid, somewhere in some way by every-one. And the last thing they offer is freedom.

This was all a part of the mechanization of art and the mechani-zation of sex.

That my father walking the grounds of the lonely drive-in and giving out free coffee on a cold May night was a part of this revolu-tion that wasn't a revolution would surprise him. But he hung on to it, to keep going. Just as he hung on to his theatre in town when there was no longer any hope. He wouldn't close it down, even if it meant it only operated three nights a week. Or two. Even if it meant he had to travel to Moncton to find what happened to a picture from Paramount or MGM that wasn't delivered because someone in a Famous Players theatre wasn't going to put it on the bus to a theatre that was not part of their cabal. Or they would put part of the movie on the bus to us—the first two reels—or the wrong movie —the movie he ran only a week before. It would circle back to him in grave hilarity, at his own expense. There he went in his car, sadly chasing these elusive reels to bring them to a theatre where every-thing else seemed to be in death throes, too. The mills were going, the air base, the mines—all was being diminished in the name of a progress we couldn't keep up with, while new television satellite dishes bloated our grey skylines, and videos replaced television programming itself.

He became a man doing a job that no longer seemed to count, while protecting the memory of his mother, who the younger generation no longer remembered. Yet he prided himself in doing; believing, I suppose, that one could kick a dead horse.

The drive-in screen blew down and he had to build a new one. He built a new canteen that still sat alone in the middle of a great, empty lot; that looked as part of a movie set as any from a thousand movies he ran. From those old Westerns, or the movies of the man on the run—which was so much a part of the American experience that it became a Canadian one.

He struggled to pay the heating bills at the theatre in town. He struggled until he operated it only three nights a week.

Now the staff at the drive-in became younger, and even more transient than before. The cooks came and went from the fryers, the projectionist changed, all was open to vagary. For a while he had the help of my younger brother, who along with a few dedicated young people steadied the ship, played dusk-till-dawns. But Duane Eddy guitar solos gave way over the intervening years to Marilyn Manson without my father really noticing. He put up the prices on hot dogs and hamburgers stingily, asking for a dime or fifteen cents more. That would keep us going, he supposed.

Then his wife, Margaret, our mother, died, and I suppose that was the end. He never drank before—ever. He began to. He never missed a night at the theatre or the drive-in—he started to. To him there was nothing much left. Maybe a million miles of film his own brother as projectionist had put through the reels, waiting for the change-over signals while smoking a Player's Filter. Now that didn't matter, either. Maybe every time he played a risqué film like *Peyton Place*, in 1958, he made sure he played some Christmas special for the nuns to come en masse and sit their bums in the seats. That was his penance, I suppose. That did not matter, either. Whatever film played there were no more trips down to Saint John to haggle with the distributors.

That my grandfather's grand piano sat in the silence, near the golden curtains of the Uptown's large screen, waiting for some maestro to play, showed the end of an age had come.

He sold out—for next to nothing. Thousands and thousands of dollars less than what he might have received. It was as if once he let go, left it behind, he did so for good. He wanted to rid himself of everything. Especially his guilt over our mother's death. After our mother died at fifty-eight years of age, what else mattered? And so, nothing did or seemed to. You see, he always thought, assumed, she would be there—for she always had been. She had stuck with him when many others would not have: a man obsessed with a business where he was never home—at the office during the day, and at the hall at night. At the end he must have realized how the business had destroyed their lives. For it had, as business will. He did not realize that until it was too late, and not being an articulate man—he never was—it was just one more thing he could not articulate. For a while he said he wanted to kill the doctor who botched the operation—for the doctor had done exactly that—but that gave way to silence and sadness.

At night he would watch videos of old movies that took him back to other days and times, of *Casablanca* and *Key Largo*, of Judy Holliday and Barbara Stanwyck, that he would watch in the semi-darkness of the den, alone—his wife dead and children now gone. Alone as he had been most of his life.

An entertainer with no one left to entertain, and all he once entertained with out of date.

The last few years of his life he actually made some friends, and knew some people. His sadness might have gone away—I am unsure if it ever really did. He took trips now and again, showed up places. He went out and played cards, and had a companion.

After he died, however, people did remember him. People wrote and told me tales of how he was the man at the theatre who had been kind to them when they were a little girl or boy—that they had lost their money and he had let them in for free, or bought them a bag of chips and a Coke; or that he caught them sneaking in and told them to go take a seat. That he was always there for them week after week—that he never was cross—or even when he was, they knew he didn't mean it. That once he went down all along the seats looking for a young girl's mitts. That you could not really not like a person like that; that in a way, inside his theatre, in those days, way back when, you could tell by his smile he was full of love.

2018

POEMS

ALDEN NOWLAN (1933–1983)

I give you smoke on the autumn air
Alders, gone fire red—
Popals long and white and bare
Near a snowy riverbed

Gin when the night is cold or dark
Wings to soar our sky
Hope and Truth in your fierce heart,
Knowledge, Love—
Goodbye

THE WINTER TESTAMENT

The snow has silenced the barn
Left its white hide across the walls
And blinded the horse
And tempered the grand illusion
That spring will ever come at all.

Outside by dark the sky is smoke
The dog, half-starved barks,
For he's chained to the hard-luck culvert
By his master gone away.

THE WINTER TESTAMENT 2

Beyond the crude window
Across the road the snow
Fills the tracks, the spruce stand is cold
Where the fisher burrows;

A rabbit followed my brother home
Sat on his boot in the dooryard;
And there was quite a hoot,
So he named it, I think, Thumper.

Found out later
The fisher had caught its scent
And scudded it all that day,
The rabbit
Bet against the odds

Just to get away.

NEWCASTLE, WINTER OF 1956

Leonard Drillon lay drunk downtown
While fire burned his house to ground
And trapped children screamed his
Name.

Next morning, Constable Billy Dunn
The one who kicked him in the groin
Called all his fuckin' family "scum,"
Shook his hand, looked ashamed
And offered to drive him home.

NOVEMBER 1977

November, the trees are still.
The black earth reminds us of a regimental
Song, and, from the hospital stack, smoke
From bandages
Touches that raw sky
Just at one white spot in the heaven
And I've come outside
For a cigarette.
(I look seventeen, though am twenty-seven)

Up in the room beyond the white curtain
Jammed with frost and the ridges of aluminum
Where the job is following a blue
Monitor,
The nurse after twelve years, eleven months,
Has become the disinterested partner in
The pain of others.
And, her patient,
My mother, has just suffered
Another botched operation,
By a cursory drunken doctor.

So many of her gender have died this way—
As wonderfully brave as they can manage in a
Room full of strangers, more interested in the
Machinery than in such struggling,
Frightened, still-beautiful bodies.

THE SPRING TESTAMENT

I go every day past the gravel bar
And walk to the church
In the April mud
Because my friends have tossed me out
And slammed the doors upon my face,
There in my worn suit
My face is lashed by crawling shame
I reckon with what I have done
That has so besmirched my family name
And humbled by my new stage of grace
Walk home alone in the setting sun.

PEG AT SEVENTEEN

My love was like a winter sparrow
The world she saw a winter land
The pulse of light on broken boughs
A flush of sun on popal stands;
The ice and drifts of a winter gale
Left sorrow in her eyes—
I remember my love when she was young,
Before winter made us wise.

CIRCUS

I have come out on a grey afternoon
To be at the circus with my son.
The man behind me with his wife and
Children laughs, as if a joke was so
Well crafted he's undone, and grabs not once
But twice, my shoulder as he grins.
So then he laughs every time the elephant
Breaks wind.
Or when the clown begins his task
Of wrestling with the ostrich,
He points his finger and chews
Popcorn, blows bubbles with his gum.
He is radiant in what I cannot see, that
Has become
Hilarious to him.

All these poor animals trying
To act gracious
Their eyes, again and again
Showing the universal
Symptom of mortification, remorse and pain
Not only for themselves but
For their harried trainers.

Finally it is over, all that unseen shame

And they have shone the spotlight
On the nineteen-year-old Armenian girl with
The peculiar Armenian name;
She's ninety feet up
Without a net, swinging free of the
Pin bar that keeps her from her death
All of this—all of this
In order to make a dollar.
And even though through the torn tent
Comes dismal blowing snow and rain
A smile never leaves her—for she takes it
As her duty.

And the man with his wife
And children,
No longer points or giggles
But finally understands enough, to shut
The fuck-up.

A TRIP TO THE OUTER ISLAND
(THE POET AS GUNSLINGER)

The gunslingers are always the age we were then—twenty-one or
    thirty-nine
Younger the killings become
Studies in dim pathology
Older and we mistake as comic the
Poignancy of
A gun well oiled worn so low.

The young gunslinger doesn't know
How much of a set-up it's been
Until he gets there
And is expected to be entertained
By laughing at pistol tricks he's
Seen before, and finally, though the .44
Is pointed at his head, won't draw
Except as last resort.

The old gunslinger counts on this, of course
When he holds open his shirt to show his scars
Which keeps the kid in his place.
The old man
Could spit in the kid's face before he'd
Choose to make a move.

In the end the old gunslinger
Won't come out of his room
And the kid from the first moment
Wanted to be home.

Yet coming onto evening both
Search the trees for wanted
Posters, both know what it's like
To be alone;

And the kid's reputation has grown, and grown
The price on his head is getting
Larger, and someday someone
He knows will get him in his back.

That's really what the old gunfighter
Is counting on smiling at.

THE JOURNEY

I sometimes wake, know
That we are not
Travelling through the night
Of snow with the train's endless rocking, the
Iced-over glitter of some obscure village lights
And my sons are with me, safe at home.

I have not, this time waking alone
Migrated anywhere.
That has really been my desire
As long as I have known journey,
Not to journey anymore.
For I have used travel like a drug
To ease pain I cannot treat
Affliction I cannot cure.

I have travelled
To places filled with dull company
Shamed by the actions of others
I have come upon
Or riotous in abandon of myself
All knowing gone.
I have stood with men
Who would murder if they could without a
Thought, and saw how others fawned about them
Greedy to be snivelling for no cause;
Or have agreed myself with those who had

No truth to please my sense
Of camaraderie in a bar.
With this comes wisdom to be alone
So wisdom is faith if not ignored.

I have long known,
That my youthful hope was dashed
Not only by my own frivolity,
But by the ill others had for me;
One who asked me favours as he hid
Behind the comments of his wife and friend.
And knowing I was honour bred
Never to answer what lie was said
But to do my duty if I could.
I have attained my life in spite of that,
Dream only of mercy, not justice at
The end; for mercy is justice after all.

But it seems this night I have lost more
Than I have ever gained
True loves lost, friends gone,
Those intolerant of my life
Contemptuous of my name.

Today my son asked me if we
Could go to that city street
Where he lay his best toy car down
Under some forgotten flower bed.
He smiled, unsure, but said he knew

The place it could be found
And wonders if it can't be far;
Tries to remember the city or the town.

"I forgot it there,"
He said. "You remember the garden with those tiny plants—?"

"Ah yes," I said, "and the smell of the great
Grey sea, the improbable sea that so far away
Had no comfort or claim for your mother you or me."

So I told him the trip
Could not be made—that journeys such
As those are ones we cannot take.
What is lost remains where it was lost,
Hope and love, camaraderie in a bar
Or honour squandered, all buried like his toy,
And the seas are cold and forbidding now
Even if our poor heart breaks.

But tonight my child is unsettled in his sleep,
Seeking that garden in Tasmania
To reclaim whatever part of him was left behind;
Toy car, or truck or Jeep.

And now and then I hear,
Against the dark and bitter slashing
His few clear words
"I found it, I found it every part."

As if the wind itself is asking;
Or telling that children's wisdom makes us pause
Their bravery makes us weep
And is carried in their laughing—
Telling that they themselves are our hope,
On cold nights that are so slowly passing.

PARTING AT THE STATION IN VÖCKLABROOK

Inge smiles and offers me money
I will never take
For having travelled from Paris
Through Austria by train to see her;
Offers it as gentle as a blessing,
Offers it with her kiss as sweet as kindness,
She knowing I have paid a week's wages
For a trip that ends as soon as it begins,
A trip hurried into blindness, Munich and night falling.
With the ticket takers
And station masters, the jurisprudent ones
All of us must deal with, all of our lives.
Their faces so clean shaven—
Those who would never take advantage of anyone,
Except some child running away in winter,
Orphan out of step with all the others,
A man who can never speak the language
And has been trying to all his life,
A woman with a pleading smile,
Or a stranger,
Yes, a stranger they can better.

WE HIT BILFERD

We hit Willie Bilferd in the mouth
The air was sharp, when he cried,
We all felt brave
When he tried to stand,
Wipe torment from his eyes.

He'd written a song about his mom,
Was on his way to take it home.
We threw him down and stepped on
It, the week after his father died.

He and his mom lived alone
Wore a bowtie in the November sun,
Face white as milk that dried
Leaves curled in a lime-rinsed drum.

Old memories pierce these forty years
Touch of cruelty in a child's glee,
Sitting solitary on the grey deck chair
Telling her of new friends he had,
But the one who liked him most was
Me.

THE LILLIPUTIAN LOOKS UP

I have lost my youth, Peg,
You know that.
Nothing more can be said
About curtains blowing
Above a register
In your house when
I visited that hard, cold night in 1968.
(Something I've written about for forty years)
Well,
A party in the dooryard
Rough and ready boys singing;
The winter snow, where the light went gold,
Grader passing on the road,
Bedroom
Smelling of love at twilight,
The kitchen—ah, the kitchen, my dear,
Of bacon, onions and wine.

THE HOUSE

My mother hated our house:
Big and empty
When night settled,
And the hallway ran from one end to the
Other.

There were never enough tables or chairs
Its smell contained the secret of endless hours
Of washing and scrubbing.
Ajax detergent after school at four o'clock

The floors were pulled apart
By callow children running.
Nothing nice ever lasted
And not a friend of hers entered.

All of this
And winter, winter, winter,
Besides.

She loathed it, as an
Anathema
And who could blame her.
The work was never done.

That last week
In the hospital
She tried to pull herself up.

Go home.

AUTUMN TESTAMENT

So on the hills to the north the sky is clear
And far away the metallic drone
Of rattling chainsaws
Cuts the evening to the bone.
Fresh ruts are visible in the snow
While the river, still glides cold and slow
Here is where the buck has moved
Sheltered by the frozen moon.
From the chop down can be seen
The doe that moves across the stream,
Muscled in her tough and dainty hide
While snow blanches her back and side.
The buck moves toward her in the cold
Swaggers its tines and lifts its nose,
Moves its tongue to taste the air,
Breathes in the doe urine lying there.
It is November so she is touched
By the heat of need and northern musk.
Hunted, hounded, while coyotes bark,
This union
Makes them heroic, in the chilling dark.

TRAVEL

We are travelling again my son and I
And he is so far from home,
Nor do either of us speak the language
Or understand the money
Though he holds the coins in his small fist
And the air has turned colder and the sky
Gone strange, the breath of phantoms
Plagues me day and night; and I am leaving behind
Bad plans, bad relations, I have been travelling half my life.
But by now they have discovered I am not so easy to defeat;
The slightest move against me will make me stop and fight
Rear-guard action, blowing dams and bridges,
Before continuing on.

Again there is this noise of evening,
The baggage picked up at the airport
Is like shouldering the weight of the thousand lost promises;
But now with my little son in my arms, we are in Amsterdam or
    Madrid,
And I think perhaps here is where
It is all going to be better.

NETWORKING

My brother-in-law needs a new piece
For his crankshaft and is sending it
From the Maritimes to Ontario,
By his brother who works in Brantford
Who will keep it for a day
And give it over to his ex-wife's husband
Who has a cousin who works in Kitchener
And can get the part from his friend
Who works in the junkyard near the highway,
And who has said:
"If you get it here by August
The boss is on vacation,
I can rifle through the whole yard after work,
Won't cost a goddamn thing."

OLD POETS ARE DOGS

(For Milton Acorn)

Old poets are dogs, Milton,
Or at least are torn apart by them,
Like Euripides;
Instructed to take poison,
Socrates;
Chased into a cellar
And put under arrest,
Ben Jonson;
Or cornered like Marlowe
Drink of wine in hand,
Never to understand the last moment
Any more than little Chatterton,
Chatting on about betrayal,
While searching the attic for arsenic—
Goldsmith mocked by lesser men,
Johnson himself
Left out in the end,
Or Dostoyevsky
Half mad and running from creditors,
On and on it goes, Dickinson, and Plath
Poets Keats or Poe, until we come to Canada
And in the blinding, blinded snow see
Lowry, Nowlan, Buckler, Lane and Layton.
You'd think, Milton, like you

They'd all have been treated,
Somewhat
Better.

BETRAYAL

Knowing that you who

I once loved

Kept a hidden document on me

I think that

Betrayal, in Dante's mind,

Was found our greatest sin,

Worse—very much,

Than the cauldron he put his sinners in.

THE MAN WHO LOVES MY CHILDREN

My friend does not have children,
But in his books he does have them—
Saves them from ice floes
Or bad things that happen,
Takes them to New York
Where he is of course instrumental,
Has never adopted children
Or really wanted to
Put that much weight upon his shoulders,
But in his books he does adopt
Cares for, tends to always,
For that's real compassion.
My friend was never on a city street
At night with a child in his arms,
The shutters locked and the lights snuffed out
Searching for medicine in a country
Where he doesn't know the language;
Not once, alone without money trying to buy milk
For his youngest, pockets of dust blowing against the darkness
But in his books I swear he has done it somewhere
Someplace, always where he should be,
Understanding, poignant,
And all that jazz;
My friend was never harsh with a son, no not he,
Nor ever put his life on the line for the son he never had,
Or sat up all night holding medicine
Watching his sick child sleep, praying that

The morning comes without pain,
Yet in his books he contrives to do just that
To prove he's done the same.
I cannot help but think of him
A village priest
Filled with impotent anger,
Wagging a sanctimonious finger at exhausted parents
Before going home to a beef stew dinner.
Still, my children know *exactly* who he is,
Ignores them on the street when passing,
Failed egoist he needs you to believe
What little we ever achieved,
Should simply be his for the asking.

WHEN YOU GET BACK FROM SICILY

Dad, when you get back from Sicily
We'll go out to the park
There is a hydrant near the elm
A swing chair in the dark
I remember the times we went there
But it won't be as much fun
For when you get back from Sicily
Autumn will have come.
They've taken the slides away now
The swing chair in the dark
Where Anton played last summer,
Has been mostly taken down
From the sad swinging pendulum
To the rusted iron bars
Or the dried-up naked gutter
Underneath the cooling stars.

LOVE

My son John has the sand of the world
In his dark-brown hair
Has travelled over the oceans at three
Holding his passport in his hand,
A small bowtie in his breast pocket.
Each day we have to pack
And go away,
His mother helps him straighten up his suit
Jacket, telling him of circuses to see and
Games to play.
He has become then the casualty of my bitter
War,
For he knows airports as well as me,
Knows how trips begin and never end,
And when he thinks I'm not looking
At certain moments in the sun,
His mirror-grey eyes search the wide
Blue sky for friends.

EMPEROR AND POET

Talk of me having it easy
Never being on my own
Taking on a *real* man's work
Since the time that I've been grown.
While you have gone to steady job
In white hat and company car,
Sniffed at those beneath you
Cringed at those above
Counted on a pension
And took your wife
To church on Sunday afternoon.
I am telling you:
Chaos creates the universe,
Invites emperor or poet in:
But each must expect no mercy, no quarter
And no helping hand.
This is the violent secret in such a fierce place
White hat or union boy
Has seldom had to face.

We all *must* take our poison in the end
Such is the destiny of Hannibal or Poe,
This axiom only the wisest know:

Any poet who goes back
To those who mocked him on the street
(Even if his children starve)

Is no better than teary Nero,
Pissing himself that last moment
In front of the disgusted centurion
He entreats.

THE GREATER TESTAMENT

(Written in honour of François Villon's *Grand Testament* of the year
of our Lord 1460)

To the boys who drank with me
All day, when I was twenty-one
Only to leave when
Night came on, in my student years
In a house without heat,
In a town at the very end of the year
Knowing my wife had left in worry and fear
And I still had a book to write
Finally by God's awful grace got sober
Such a career as mine is humbly dedicated.

To the girl
Who also left—She might know
By the empty student hall and turned to go
The other way, down beneath the stairs
It's now been forty years
Such a career as mine is humbly dedicated.

To the boys in Spain,
Who mocked me forty days (one is always
Mocked by lesser men)
Boys whose arms I put down in ten seconds
Their clever girlfriends' eyes suddenly playing
Dice with excuses
Such a career as mine is humbly dedicated.

To those who came to rob me in the night
Sent out by their murderous cousins
They who ran back into the street
When I came to meet them on the stairs
Such a career as mine is humbly—
Dedicated.

To the literati long ago
From my river—To that literati
Long ago—from my river—

To the wanderers in London

The New Yorker gone to Spain

The chic Europeans in Paris at the bar
The young fresh-faced
Tattooed Austrian Nazis on the train
Going nowhere
Or at any rate to Munich,

The prostitutes in Sydney, Australia, standing in the rain
Who smiling patted John Thomas on the head,
Or to those in the days of my youth who
Died, Emerson and the rest
So all the intervening years seem
Monstrous farce, mixed with grievous blame
Such a career as mine is humbly dedicated.

But to you two most of all—
Who dismissed our friendship; spoke out against us
Smeared my name, who pissed in our face
And called it rain.

As if betrayal was a thing on which you could take pride,
Be known,
When my wife and children and I were most alone,
To you two most of all,
Such a career as mine is humbly dedicated.

PLAYING THE INSIDE OUT

I WILL SPEAK A BIT TODAY OF THE INNER CIRCLES IN WHICH literary matters are discussed, and literary reputations made or broken. I will also speak of an idea that was prevalent when I was young and, in some ways, still is: that to be a writer, one must take on the conventional and, in doing so, be a renegade.

From the first moment I became aware of this ideal, I was also aware of the pretense often involved in assuming this, or assuming what the conventional was or wasn't, or should or shouldn't be. And that, in most ways, the real writers among us, or at least the writers I most admired, were outsiders, because they were not considered trendy or radical; that is, they had no talent to play the game of outsider and therefore most often were.

I am an old man, so I can say what I want.

Which addresses my opening point.

If people wait until they are old men or women to say what they want, then it is probably a good assumption that they have never said what they wanted to say before and, in the end, they will not.

Those who cannot give their opinion as young men and women, in spite of the consequences, will never do so as old men and women, for fear of the consequences.

So many grab on to each new bit of knowledge as real knowledge and, like Anna Scherer in *War and Peace*, are predictably in vogue at all times.

Predictably is the word.

This necessity to always be in fashion—to be *au courant* or *avant-garde*—is what dooms writers and their writing to the prevalent and the superficial. It is, to paraphrase Matthew Arnold, a truth for the moment, rather than a truth for all time. The truth for all time is different—much harder to arrive at because it almost always needs to be retold with each passing generation—and is almost never in fashion when it is. We must, as Robert Browning suggests, fight against the misapprehension of the age.

No age has had more misapprehension than this one. No age has been more certain of itself in ways that blind itself and its more susceptible writers to what is simply current or fashionable.

Some of the finest people I know, who think for themselves, have never once acted outrageous or rebellious or joined in the sometimes bogus urgency for empowerment. Unfortunately many writers and academics I have known feel that this idea of a character's empowerment is the one prerequisite to showing independence against some despotic identity. This might be fine if they treated the idea of empowerment with the actual dignity it deserves.

An episode in the popular hospital television series *House* is specific on this. A young intern, certain that the eccentric Dr. House will accept him because he has long hair and a tattoo (so therefore must be an individual fighting against the system), is told by the doctor, "If you want an example of people who really don't care what others think, look at the Asian student who studies at the library for fourteen hours a day—that is real rebellion." Although this is an easy truism and is arguable, it still has something relevant to say about the larger issue of people thinking inside the box while claiming to be outsiders and blaming all "convention" on others.

When I was a boy, it was embarrassing to listen to older people suddenly waxing enthused about the ideas and intentions of the young—fifty-five-year-old men suddenly growing their hair (the fashion of kids when I was eighteen), wearing love beads and talking in the language of youth to show how they were now independent of ideas that had once inhibited them. This is what Princess Hélène, the unfaithful, overindulged wife in *War and Peace*, has her husband, Pierre, do in 1812, convincing him to grow his sideburns, though the poor man looks ridiculous. This sounds trite. But being in vogue as a writer can be every bit as trite as Princess Hélène, and it took Pierre, a man with a great, great soul, half the novel to break free.

When I was a young man starting my career, the transparency and false courage of adopting a supposed radical ideology was often, but not always, lost on those succumbing to it. The poetry journals published in my youth are filled with this kind of painful self-indulgence that comes from a notional idea of the world, rather than life experience. What is most arresting is the fact that within these journals, the real poets stand out amid all this angst-filled quasi-radicalism with true poetical perception and force.

Alden Nowlan once mentioned the poet Brian Bartlett, whose writing appeared in one of these journals long ago: "I knew he was for real," Nowlan told me, "because he was a kid of sixteen and was the only one perceptive enough to write about being one." That is, by being himself and knowing it, he didn't have to join. Or, more tragically, perhaps he couldn't.

The great thing about Bart Simpson is his ability to reveal to us the scandal of popular sycophancy, while using Homer as the unassuming foil for modern ambivalence. I will paraphrase a certain scene:

"Dad," Bart says in the episode where, to fit in, he saws the head off the statue of Jeb Springfield, "what should we do to fit in and be liked by popular people?"

Homer reflects: "Son, we should do everything we can—for the most important thing, no matter what, is to be popular."

Then he adds suspiciously, "You haven't murdered anyone, have you?"

"No."

"Good—anything else is fine."

Exaggeration makes the point. It is safer, of course, not to take a stand alone: to be perceived as different while the whole notion of our joining in promotes our inclusion. This is, of course, the one real slavery—the kind C. S. Lewis warned about in his essay "The Inner Ring"—the kind of inner circle that Solzhenitsyn wrote about in his novel *The First Circle*. It was exposed by Tolstoy in *War and Peace*. The idea of the inner circle is with us always—men and women striving to belong to the most significant group and often, sometimes in very overt ways, giving up their own ideals and even humanity along the way, in order to make this happen. The group itself is irrelevant; we have all been tempted to give up at least a part of ourselves in order to belong. It doesn't matter whether we are a mechanic, a surgeon or an artist.

The significant commonality is the willingness to accommodate our values in order to belong to a group of others who might object to the values we hold, while hoping for a time in the future when we may say our piece without fear of retribution from those to whom we now belong. If writers do this—and many of my generation do—sooner or later it will damage their art (and it often does), even if it promotes their career. It will damage their art in ways so subtle it may not be known right away. But it will be seen over time.

Any false statement provoked not in error but by a willingness to forgo our own sense of truth in order to bond with a group truth that is socially prevalent or powerful will be known sooner or later. We witness it at dinner parties and ignore it, this conceit in spouting the current wisdom, whether we believe in it or not. To see it in a book is glaring.

What is more glaring, as the philosopher René Girard writes, is whom we manage to scapegoat in order to hold on to prevalent wisdom. And this, I suppose—the scapegoating of those who cannot for one reason or another join—is the graver and deeper sin. It is the only thing that I have ever tried to warn young people, who want to write, against. It is a very hard thing to warn against, for the idea that one should comply with strong and socially accepted views weighs heavily upon the young. Especially when such views come from the learned at university and are seen, by people one admires, as being necessarily far-reaching.

As Nietzsche says, "men believe in the truth of that which is plainly strongly believed." Many of the views strongly believed today have become a mantra for our literary society, because it is also assumed that a literary society is "proactive" in a way that is accepted within the parameters of a left-of-centre ideology. To some, it is absolutely absurd to refute this or to look at life as being positive by looking at it in any other way. Those who do are sooner or later cast out. When they are cast out, they are not called "renegades." They are called "conventional"; whereas those who hold on to the mantra are called "original."

This is particularly distressing when one comes from an area of the world that is looked upon as conventional anyway—the Maritimes. It sometimes puts us at a double disadvantage. If we try to write truthfully about our own experience to say it is as wondrous and as human as anyone else's, we come into the centre of the ring already one eight-count down. Or at least we did when I was a youngster.

At first glance, it seems not too much of a problem to join with other professionals, who seem more worldly than we are. And perhaps it is so seamless that you feel you have always belonged. And if you agree with the opinions of the group, then you do. Yet many opinions are reshaped to fit the prevailing ones. And the opinions of groups are often notional rather than experience based. And this is a dangerous problem: the problem of assumption rather than truth.

"Whatever else poetry is freedom. / Forget the rhetoric, the trick of lying / All poets pick up sooner or later," Irving Layton warns. He is right. But he is not only making a statement here. He is also revealing a condition. Poetry *is* freedom. It has to be, to be poetry. Therefore you must guard it as you would freedom. I will paraphrase what Alice Munro, speaking to my good friend Jack Hodgins, said one night: "They talk about the writing family—I have no idea what that means—a writer is on her own."

She is right. Margaret Laurence spoke of a writing "breed," which I believe cannot exist and remain true at the same time. It is an oxymoron, of course, but one to which we should pay close attention. Joining with a volley of strong, seemingly worldly opinion and becoming included with famous people is a vague and elusive kind of attraction to a young person.

Yet, as Munro and Layton suggest, joining in a group dynamic may be tantamount (and I said *may* be—I am not saying it always *is*) to giving up your ethical or literary values for a powerful group value and is really self-imposed bondage. No real harm can come to your work if you refuse it, as writers and musicians and artists like Beethoven and Dostoyevsky and Keats and Hardy and Brontë and Picasso and Eudora Welty refused it. But it is not easy. For harm can come to your reputation and peace of mind. If you are not what is seen to be correct, you are seen to be in error. So it is, in many ways, the hardest and most necessary thing an artist, man or woman, can ever do. At some point, you must turn away. If and when you do, you are seen to being doing such; and that is never lost on those who have a whimsical idea of attachment as priority.

I am directing my talk to the young writer, of course. Only you can decide when you are true to yourself as an artist or have slid to those who want you to change yourself for what they think is acceptable. Or to find out what is acceptable, knowing that some-day it will be of value. What we say that is acceptable to ourselves is the question—it is the voice of our own moral compass pointing true north. To change the compass bearing in ourselves to please the more popular conceit is to *know*, even if others do not detect it right away.

I suppose that when I was writing as a young kid from what was considered backwoods Maritimes, most of the really popular con-ceptions of literature, and more importantly the categories in which people were viewed, came to me from away. So from the very first, the popular conceptions of what literature and even freedom *was* tended to alienate me, as did many of the works called "brilliant" from central Canada or New York. Perhaps that is why I think this conversation important. Nor am I saying there is only one way to write, or that some of these works weren't brilliant. But I am suggesting to the young writer that there is one way to write for *you*, and no one can do this *but* you. So many times the real rural landscape of my youth was dismissed by writers who were considered important and dazzling.

It is the only advice I, as a middle-aged man, have to give. Most of those "brilliant" novels that came to me by way of urban life did not seem to understand what I knew about working-class men and women when I was fifteen. But many university profs later told me that these books *did* and not to think so was an error on my part.

So even before I ever finished writing a book, I was told I was in error. And if I had believed I was in error, not one of my books would have been written. This was a crisis faced when I was twenty and twenty-one, and though the world has changed and the Maritimes are no longer looked upon the way they once were, it is what I believe other young men and women, no matter where they are from, will sooner or later have to face.

It is much better to believe in leftist ideology, for instance, if those on a committee that might get you something believe that is what writing should promote. And if this is the test you come up against, it is more than a symbolic one if it changes an opinion about a character that might be in conflict. Even a modest realignment of a novel's intention for personal comfort can make a writer forgo true art. We are not all heroes, like Roark in Ayn Rand's *The Fountainhead*— where Rand took on the problem of an artist refusing convention even if this convention made him famous. At times, this novel is achingly oversimplified so that Rand can make her point. But the point is made. And all in all, it is as true now as it was then. Or was when Alden Nowlan praised Brian Bartlett for not succumbing to the fashionable self-consciousness of his more hip and with-it friends.

Yet, standing up for one's art is a nebulous kind of engineering of one's own soul and is therefore difficult to write about now. Nor does everyone feel uncomfortable within groups that preach a common destiny for politics in literary culture. Yet, in some ways, I really believe the best writers do, and in many ways, have had to face it all of their lives. And the great painters and the great musicians, too. They have had to stand up against the odds in ways unimaginably painful and for so little gain it seems fruitless to continue on the line of their true compass.

But *seems* is the word.

When Beethoven was writing his greatest symphony, he was reviled, hated, called "an abuser of women and children." His lawyer and his nephew thought he was mad—and wanted him imprisoned, as an embarrassment. Since he was going deaf and blind, all he could utter to them was "da da da da, da da da da, da da da da, da dada!" Which proved to them his encroaching imbecility, yet became, of course, the signature moment of the Ninth Symphony's "Ode to Joy." Can I say that if he was not condemned, not reviled, not thought of as mad, he might never have composed the greatest piece of music ever? One does not necessarily include the other, and to say so is false romanticism. But by the time he wrote this symphony, he was jubilantly mocked as a failure by musicians he had disagreed with most of his life. They exulted in his failure, both personal and professional, and had driven spikes into the heart of his reputation. How many of us, in our comfortable perches preaching artistic greatness, would spend one night like him in order to accomplish what he did? What I am saying, of course, is that he did not want to be in this position, either—he did not wish to be reviled and mocked on the street, hated by his own blood. But he would not and could not forgo the demands of his own creative conscience to create in some safer way. If that is a drastic example, it is not a qualitative exception.

It is somewhat true that Beethoven himself becomes the poster boy for what many well-thought-of Canadian and American novels (and the mountains of theory about those novels) have preached concerning the one-dimensional violent male in our society from the 1970s on. In fact, in many books, the male is viewed in no other way, especially a working-class male. And Beethoven is the poster boy. Not in what he wrote or how his heart was, but at certain times in how he acted. He is, or at times was, looked upon as deeply flawed in his humanity, of course.

Except for the "Ode to Joy."

And there, for the entire field of today's sometimes precious literary semantics, lies the rub. I am simply suggesting that a character like a Beethoven must be written about like a Beethoven. But to say this, to certain professors and writers back when I began to write, was to be seen in error.

For some reason, back when I began to write, and for years and years, critics believed that violence was most often one-dimensional, and always male, and therefore easy to define and fight against. A certain kind of male was the "authority figure," whom we must be against and therefore write against. Priests, of course, but working males, businessmen, executives, as well. Therefore, for sophisticated people, the guilty were always quite easy to define. What was worse is that far, far too many educated people were comfortable with this. In affluent, intellectual, urban Canada, it was a means of categorizing people, and this, too, was seen as correct. The only problem was that some of these texts knew nothing about violence: how it developed and worked not only overtly but coercively or covertly. And some of the violence people were against and aghast at was nothing more than actual physical labour. Physical labour was often misunderstood and despised, and so the characters that did it were, as well.

Looking back, I realize that for a long time, my own work was not considered successful because I did not agree with those who had attached so much importance to what they thought my work should say. I seemed on the wrong side of the fence. My work was physical and seemed violent. My work seemed misogynistic, degrading to women. My work seemed, as a good friend once lamented, too working class. But worst of all, to him and to others, my work was outside the realm of the university and seemed anti-intellectual.

Of course, *seems* is the word.

Seems is an important word in the literature of all men and women from Shakespeare to Emily Dickinson. Shakespeare uses *seems* as does Milton. Both use it to show a counterfeit in our midst. *Seems* is the word that plays like a water strider across the consciousness of all good men and women, to change what seems like, to actually be. "Seems to be violent" may not be violent—and "seems to be concerned and considerate" may be, looking closer, trifling and sanctimonious.

In Milton's *Paradise Lost,* what seems to be, when Beelzebub and Satan meet in Hell, or when Eve is tempted, never really is. Seems is an approximation or a perversion of a great truth that becomes, over time, an outright lie that can be savage and deadening. Savage and deadening—a bit harsh, perhaps? But if we change our land-scape, or characters, or the intended meanings and humanity of those characters on small matters in order to belong, we will lack the necessary courage to deliberate on the important ones that take us outside these groups to true art.

I have discovered over the last number of years that if I am a writer, then I am supposed to be like-minded and in sync with other writers in Canada. Supposedly we all want the same things. I have let-ters from PEN, and from the Writers' Union and the Canada Council for the Arts, that state this. And maybe this is even true. Who knows? Maybe we do want the same things. But maybe we have to arrive at the things we all want differently, by our own road, so to speak. And I also suppose this is what everyone says they want.

Yet once I became well known, some then believed I would be like-minded. That I would look upon the world that treated my people so much differently than the more urban and sophisticated world others came from, and still I would be like-minded. That is, have the same ideas about my world that they who didn't know my world did. The idea that if you are well known, you should be like-minded is a rather powerful one in literary circles today. Why would you be well known if you are not like-minded?

"Imagine what can be done when like-minded people get together," the husband of a very famous writer once wrote to me.

Well, yes, as I pointed out, I can imagine, and I have not thought it necessary to join. I tell you, if I was like-minded with any writer in this country or any other, I would never have written *Blood Ties*, or *For Those Who Hunt the Wounded Down*, *Lives of Short Duration* or *Mercy Among the Children*, nor would I have been able to conceive of writing them. For parts of all of my novels, good or bad, come from a belief that if I were holding to any group's theories about these books or the characters in these books, my intentions would then have to be altered or dismissed.

But there is something else that bothered me. It is this: the idea that like-minded people are somehow good people who are forcing needed change in the world, and these needed changes must be explained within the context of a literary work—so much so, that these needed changes should be fostered upon my characters themselves. I have discovered that this is almost always a misshaping of the phrase "like-minded people" and a misrepresentation of art. There are needed changes, of course. I know that. Who am I to say there are not?

But I have learned that the needed changes some espouse tirelessly are the very ones that would categorically deny that the world I grew up in and write about has virtue. That the rural world I write about has value in the way I demand it in my books, regardless of the flaws and on occasion because of the flaws of that world. As I have mentioned, what was considered one of the biggest flaws of that world was physical labour, which many in the insulated urban world did not investigate or understand.

The idea was that if I was a trouper—a good fellow—I would essentially show in my work that I wanted these people to change—that I would want Cecil in *Blood Ties* to change and Leah to transform in a way that would make them, well, responsible, in a middle-class way. And by being middle class, they would then know how to be more acceptable and have a more progressive value system. I am speaking here of my own experience because it is what I know.

Yet, I have come to the realization that many Maritime writers have dealt with the same thing and have been dealt the same blows, for we still—or at least in my generation—lived in a world where we wrote about our traditions as being at least not more negative than other so-called systems.

I believe this is the truth about the best work of Nowlan, MacLeod, Buckler, Trethewey and others. I do not think this is comparable in any other part of the country. I believe there are many reasons for this, the very least of which is backwardness. But it is in some circles (or, at least, was back when I was younger)—and in some powerful literary circles of critics and publishers—looked upon as backwardness and sometimes as ignorance and prejudice.

Of course, Nowlan and MacLeod, Buckler and Trethewey, and younger writers like Ken Harvey and Joel Hines, are really just the opposite of backwardness, or prejudice, or ignorance. Their worlds reflect a healthy scepticism of power (both chauvinist and feminist), an unusual kindness for the underdog, a real pursuit of equality among men and women and a dislike of notional knowledge rather than knowledge gained from hard-earned experience. Much of today's writing says, in fact, that this is what it is after, and yet so little of it has the power of earned experience found in the books of Trethewey, Nowlan, Harvey, Hines, MacLeod or Buckler. Many of these writers have in their own lifetimes been derisively dismissed and, at times, scapegoated. Yet, few writers who have dismissed them can equal their power and their, as Oscar Wilde calls it, "instinct for life." One CBC writer said to me onstage that only a writer who has lived should write—that is, a writer older than I was at the time of my earliest books. Anyone who thinks this knows little or nothing about writing, or what lived experience entails.

We might realize that the two funniest writers in English Canada, both Atlantic writers, Herb Curtis and Wayne Johnston, have never won the Leacock Medal Award for Humour. Why? It is probably because their work is considered vulgar, because it is utterly human. Besides this, both writers have an unseen quality. Just as Nowlan most often knew in his poems what was true, both Curtis and Johnston know what is actually funny. You have to actually know what is funny to be funny—or to judge what is funny.

Those who cannot judge what is funny will have no more success in judging what is truly tragic. Much of what is considered tragic in Canadian letters is simply the reinforcement of what is considered politically incorrect by today's comfortable and intellectualized middle class.

The essays of Wayne Curtis (who is the brother of Herb Curtis) are some of the finest written in English Canada, and they are often dismissed because they seem so ordinary.

Yet, their instinct for life at times far surpasses those that have won awards.

There is another problem I wish to briefly address. It is the more terrible problem, if you will. A scapegoat is almost always needed to ensure collaboration within a group. If the group is one that believes inherently that literature must be part of urban social activism and that good literature is politically correct literature (still, in some way, a prevalent ideology in central Canada and the United States, certainly throughout the seventies and eighties), then those who don't seem to be writing in the vein of urban social activism will be scapegoated. Especially if their refusal of social activism initially seems, as Nowlan's and MacLeod's did, to be in direct conflict with the prevailing status quo.

You see, this is the secret: no matter what group, body or institution, there are always exclusions. That is fine, of course, until we use the fact that they don't belong in order to dishonestly or boorishly keep from them that which they might very well deserve.

There was no Governor General's Award for *The Lost Salt Gift of Blood*.

Well, there was no Nobel Prize for Count Leo Tolstoy.

Like children in a tree house, we decide who is a member of our club and who is not. At first it is wonderful to be in the tree house— for we are the only four or five allowed. But sooner or later we see that the dimensions have enclosed us and the only way out is down. The real problem with this group is that some only have the talent to stay where they are.

But the powerful allure of the tree house cannot be underestimated. For it is here that any member can wield real power over better men and women, who are refused entrance in one way or another. And critics and literary committee members, who judge awards and give grants, have often and will always exercise blind power over the writer and the artist, who in the end will be seen to have been wiser and better.

That, as C. S. Lewis affirms, is the secret Boris discovers in *War and Peace*, where, because of connections, he is invited to a meeting with Prince Andrei while a decorated general is forced to wait outside. He plays it much to his own benefit: realizing that to be inside gives you power over others no matter your own worth or talent. Yet, what hundreds of men in the Politburo, who later died, discovered with Comrade Stalin was that the more of your soul you give up to get into the circle of power, the less there is of you once you gain entrance.

To be like-minded to the point where the ideas you wanted to express about your characters in your great novel or great symphony cannot now be expressed, for fear of harming your relationship with those you rely upon for security, is to carve away part of your being. I am only saying: be aware that if you rely upon others and comply with their determination or doctrine of truth, you will someday no longer have the qualities that protect you from mistaking what others demand from your art as artistic virtue. And slowly it will hamper you in deciding the artistic virtue of others.

The truth of so-called like-minded people and artistic virtue, whether in 1970 when I was a boy or today, becomes interchangeable. It is one and the same, and you will end up seeking what others do in order to belong, in order not to be singled out and scapegoated . . . so your work will not be bloodied and dismissed. Am I foolish enough to say this happens to everyone who joins in common theory? No, but this is the tendency.

There are two characters in Solzhenitsyn's *The First Circle* who epitomize this tendency. One is a writer, much applauded at the time by Stalin. In the Soviet Union, his novels are considered masterpieces. He has a large apartment and a good life for his wife and child. Only he knows he is not saying what is in his heart. Yet, each time he starts to write the "real novel," the one he believes he is destined to write, he feels as if Stalin is standing behind him watching. So he begins to change his novel slightly each and every time. And each and every time he says, "My next novel will be the book where I tell the truth."

The second is a character in the Lubyanka prison. He, along with other intellectuals, is asked to make a voice-deciphering machine in order to facilitate the arrest of a man the NKVD—People's Commissariat for Internal Affairs—knows has made a phone call in an attempt to warn an enemy of the state. The prisoner is a brilliant scientist and is able to make this machine to catch this man for Stalin, but there is one problem. He is free. How is this prisoner free? Because Stalin's henchmen made a mistake—they took from him everything in his life he counted on and hoped for. Gone were his wife, children, house and job. Gone was his name and reputation. Now, standing before the warden in this prison, who needs a favour from him, it is he, not the warden, not the writer of the so-called masterpieces, not Stalin himself, who is free. This is a strange way to gain this kind of freedom. But it is the kind of freedom a writer should try to aspire to. It is every bit as hard as a drinker giving up his bottle in order to become free. There might be unimaginable dark nights of the soul.

You see, it is not whom the groups include as kindred spirits but whom they have excluded. Rarely have we failed to exclude someone who, as an artist, does not deserve to be excluded and, in fact, deserves more applause than most. To say this is not an unspoken tenet in popular culture is not to see how popular culture censors itself to the point where real truth is suspect, just as the truth Alden Nowlan gave us was largely suspect, while he was living, by many who now call him their "favourite poet."

What many in the realm of our prominent literary social milieu sometimes fail to realize is that all great books are political and almost all political books fail to be great.

When I was a young man, I wore a name tag, and went to conferences, and became aware of this hidden exclusionary clause in some of the more notable literary figures present. And unfortunately, as I have briefly mentioned, the people they were excluding were also being blamed, in one way or another, for many of the modern social ills that they themselves wished to write about and unravel. The people who were held responsible I could call "rednecks." I could call them "white trash." I could call them (as one of my characters was called by one person on the CBC) "illiterate brawlers." And I might, in a way, blame him and others. However, having grown up with people like this character, the one thing I did not have was a policy of singling them out for blame in order to exonerate myself or my intellectual class or ever to dismiss their humanity to do such.

Write what you must, but don't try to reach the safe shore by jumping into waters you are unlikely to navigate. Don't write about the rural world to please an urban sensibility if you come from rural Canada. Don't ever tell people that what they want to hear is what they should hear—for the good of literature. To the extent that this has ever been done in Canadian literature, it is a tragedy.

"Whatever else, poetry is freedom," Layton says, and we must hold to that come hell or high water.

What I am saying to the young writer is never fear that you, too, will be evaluated most harshly in your life for telling the truth. Know that the truth, not as others see it, but as you do, can only be told by you. And if you do it well enough, it not only sets you free but your characters, as well. It brings to the world myth and grace. The most important gift you can give the world is your right to write how you feel, not how others who seem to be more important tell you how you should feel. There are no guarantees if you do this, but there is no hope if you do not.

One thing: like Nowlan, Trethewey, Buckler and MacLeod, you will never have to play the inside out. If you attempt to tell the truth about your world—as only you see it, the compassionate truth that the world of the artist needs—you will almost certainly be an outsider sooner or later, and at times it will be much, much lonelier than the part of the outsider that is often glibly played within those special centres without either sacrifice or meaning.

2007

AUGUST 1955

LACE CURTAINS BLEW FORWARD IN THE HEAT OF THE SMALL
bedroom, and I remember a kind of midsummer ennui—a word I
did not know then, or for years after, but there it was nonetheless.
Outside at the yard's edge a fury of small hot dust storms blew up
near the cracked, chalked sideway; where the girl next door, wearing her white ankle socks, had practised her hopscotch with a piece
of heavy, blood-coloured glass, telling us of the great circus up the
street and across the back fields and beyond the warehouses at the
top of town. And so hearing this we went back into the house, to ask
our mother's permission.

It would be a giant coup if permission was granted, being this
was a circus, and being my brother was five and I was four. Not that
at this age we had not done things that would make parents wilt,
but this was a circus, a carnie, a place where outsiders came and
worked, and moreover took money from children, and our mother
did not trust them. Also, it was in direct competition with our family
theatre, which always ceased to run matinees during circus week

because our seats would never be occupied. It seemed like a betrayal. That is, our theatre closed, the cement steps keeping time to blank glass doors, the heated bricks redundant and lost and stilled, while customers dressed for the evening, came and went on sidewalks, drifting along toward a foreign threat to our livelihood. Stillness, I suppose, was the word, our sheets proclaiming the place was now closed.

There was a stillness in our bungalow, too, that hot afternoon; the monotonous tick of the clock and the vague, indiscernible soundlessness of the town in the midst of listless August adding to this stillness. Within this was the kind of moment when the air itself conspires melancholy that you feel in closeness on your skin. There was the faint sound of jazz from the radio, the sweet and distant trumpets of cities we did not know, complemented slightly by the dripping of the kitchen tap.

It seemed as if no one at all was home.

But things had been like this for days because our father was working at the office and our mother was ill. She could get up for a while, but exhaustion would force her back to bed, and she lay in the room with the lace curtains billowing softly in midsummer, her beautiful chestnut hair on a pillow; lying on her side in her housedress as my brother approached. I suppose at that moment she was young enough to be my daughter now. Strange how time passes so easily—and remembering her hopes, tragically, so that moment and a thousand others have come and gone back into eternity; wherever that may be; poured outward moment by inevitable moment to a cosmos that might be best described by some movie still, a shadow along a wall, a face in a crowd passing by Jean-Paul Belmondo in Paris in 1960.

Her resolution was strong against it, but my brother's resolution was stronger still. And knowing that we had been left alone that summer, that we had sat for hours on steps overlooking our driveway, or sat in our veranda where bric-a-brac collected dust, she relented—though my brother had to promise to keep my hand; that he was never to talk to strangers, and we had to come home in an hour. Besides this, we had to change our clothes. So she got up with not a little difficulty and went to the dresser to make sure we had clean pants and shirts, and socks.

There in our bedroom dark enough, with the curtains drawn to the conspiracy of afternoon heat, we had to put on clean, pressed shorts and shirts, and socks. Which seemed to me even then (if she was worried about kidnappers) slightly incongruous, for wasn't she making us more attractive to them, whoever these kidnappers were? Well, that was her way—cleanliness, come what may.

Still it is as clear to me now as it was years ago, sitting on the bed to change my socks to go off to a circus that fifteen minutes before I had not known existed. A great adventure awaiting us as surely as all the other children who had been fortunate enough to go. And the vague feeling that this was not quite right, for it was permission granted because our mother was ill. And there was one more thing. When we came out to the kitchen, our mother confessed that she had no money. She kept looking through her purse nervously, but was unable to find a cent. She sat at our metallic kitchen table with a change purse in her hand, worried that now we might not be able to go; that our hopes had been dashed—and she knew something about the world of dashed hopes. This made her search more relentlessly.

Like ourselves I do not think she knew what circuses cost. But the secret was becoming revealed to me, then and there. I discovered by this search that I only wanted to go because my brother wished to. And our mother was trying to find some money so my brother could entertain me. All of this hidden desire, one for the other, seemed to dissipate into the flat, still air without a word being said.

Finally looking in the drawer beneath the phone book, she found a quarter.

And so cleaned and pressed, and with a quarter in my brother's pocket, we started out the door.

When we came outside, the heat hit us full force. There was no one on the street, or on any of the interconnected streets beyond. It was silent and hot. The girl had gone, her hopscotch over, her blood-coloured piece of glass like a burnt pebble.

Viewed from above, like all children are—from the air above our heads, we were solitary on a long, bent, broken street, with houses and yards, and gardens and fences.

I followed my brother, as he tugged my hand. Up toward the circus we went, beyond the field where they played ball, beyond the tension wires and the new telephone poles, beyond the houses my grandmother once built—beyond the lane leading off to the station, and the creosote poles lying by the railway tracks. And we kept going, beyond the warehouse, with stingers grown up its sides, where winos sat and called to us. Then turning along the path so we would not be seen by the Hurleys—who were my brother's enemies; he thinking I did not realize this—and then toward the smell of grease and fries, and litter, and tents, the sound of barkers and the sound of static, somehow obscenely happy music.

It cost a quarter to get in, and the lady, severe in her red kerchief, told us this—the heat making her more unwilling to relent. It seemed in fact to me that she was more than delighted to tell us. Where was she from, with her grey leathery skin? And where was her next stop? Another town a little way away, with the same children searching for a quarter?

We started home along the side path, my brother still holding my hand. Then at the Tilt-A-Whirl motors he ducked under the rope, and we were in. We came to the rides, and found out that rides cost a quarter apiece.

"You can go on one," I said to my brother at the merry-go-round.

"No," he said. "We will find a ride we can go on together."

But we could not find such a ride—nothing at all. Every ticket was a quarter. So after an hour we were standing in the middle of the grounds, he still clutching my hand.

"You go on a ride," I said, feeling I was holding him back, and at any other time he would not be guilty.

Yet he was determined not to. And I began to realize why. He was under obligation because our mother was ill. This is when my heart went out to him.

"No—we will get two candy apples," he said. And we went to the candy apple stand.

"We can only have one," he said.

"Well, we will share it," I said.

But he did not want to do that. In a kind of taciturn fury—a furnace of anger on a hot day—he stared at the adults around him as if they were betrayers of innocence, as if in his hope they had betrayed not only him but his mother and me.

I am sure he did not think of it like that, but I am just as sure this is what he thought it was. Somewhere in his heart a pact of some kind, between small children and the outside world, had been broken—and he would not break his pact with me, even though he was the one who had thought of the circus, and I wanted him to. He stood off to the side a resolute little man, holding my hand, with a determined and subtle valour.

"I don't want anything anyway," I said.

"We will keep the quarter for later—and go downtown," he said.

"There is lots of stuff we can get downtown."

We turned toward home.

Our mother was anxiously looking out the window as we trudged back down the street hand in hand, a brother who on another occasion had thrown me in horseplay over his head and busted my collarbone. We told our mother nothing of these events, as trifling as they seemed.

I have long given up the notion that our disappointment was anyone's fault—at the little circus or anywhere else. Still I will not give up the notion of a child's bravery and love in a moment so fleeting it goes for the most part unrecognized, unless you are a child at heart yourself.

SCAPEGOATS

THE FIGHTING OF BULLIES HAS ALWAYS INTERESTED ME. FIRST because I knew so many of them, and second because at times they were uncharacteristic in their approach. Or I might clarify this by saying that society has different ways to enable and reward intimidation that in essence it needs in order to remain a society. The idea of bullies being thugs and punks has a rather one-dimensional application. Not many of us think of sophisticates or academics as bullies. Yet most of them have had some leaning toward it—if not they would never have fit in. They may or may not have been geeks in high school—but they had their eye on the prize, and so often the prize was to become safe and snug, and accepted.

It is really the need to fit in that creates the bully. That is why they can often be seen as a parcel standing around and gawking at one who is alone.

In the university common rooms where I sat in the early eighties, the idea of fitting in was essential for those seeking tenure, and so the idea of holding predetermined opinions that may disagree with the opinions of those chairs who had the authority to offer you a job became very brave or very foolhardy. So, often people suppressed what they thought or how they felt, in order to maintain a decorum that was wholly or partly false. Falsehood is recognized as a lack of virtue, so I believe universities become institutions without virtue, teaching generations of young adults. Compliant students catch on to this, and succumb in various degrees—sometimes giving up their own ideas and ideals and opting instead for the sophist's mantra that all is open to question. Therefore one does not have to suffer unduly for holding any value if all is open to question, for the value you hold is open to question, as well. And therefore it can become very tedious to others if you proclaim it too much.

This is what I discovered to be the endemic sophistry at the university level. Yes, all is open to question—except university cant and bullying and sophistry. If you question that, you become the outsider in the great union of freethinking men and women who often quibble for years over a chair or position.

I found that there is also an unindicted co-conspirator in all of this, and it happens to be the learned public, who on the one hand deplores lack of thought and on the other hand lacks the judgment to really think for themselves. The idea of their children going to university and in the end exhibiting much of the same wise folly of their professors becomes something natural and desired for hordes of people. The notion that people cannot think if they do not have a university degree is a spellbindingly popular one among much of the middle class, who insist our children go there. Does this mean I think university is a waste of time? Not at all! University at its best is a place of wonder and enlightenment, and I have never excoriated that. I am simply addressing the act of bullying in this world as well as others. And life away from university has the exact same pitfalls and I am simply saying our youth must be aware of all of this.

Because on the other hand there are thousands and millions of us who grew up among people who for years thought that anything to do with learning was discredited by "real people," who had no time to study or to learn. The real people supposedly were real because they did not know, learn or particularly want to; were surly if actual book learning was mentioned as an ideal. They became shills for a society that laughed a great deal at great knowledge.

I find that both of these camps, both the intellectual and the anti-intellectual, can have a common trait, and that is an unwitting eagerness for the adherents never to think independently. I have seen it and registered it many times over the course of my writing. I have seen how, by these same people, outsiders are often targeted. I know as well as you that the examples are too many to count. I was sent to a physiatrist because I wanted to write, and strapped by the principal, expelled from school. My parents, as good as they were, were frightened lest I do something outside the social norm, worried what others might say.

But that was minor. I finished writing my first novel and published it at twenty-three.

Others were far less fortunate. We can think of Ashley Smith as the more terrible case, a girl caught throwing crabapples, and never to leave prison. An example of the pure mendacity of schooled ignorance, petty jurists and rigid, uncompromising witlessness that comes in part—yes, from a doctrinaire education and a social milieu that craves acceptance. Oh yes, she was no angel. Yes, she had problems. Yes, she did not fit. Still, what kind of bullying by society at every level did she experience? What kind of neglect, by unthinking *knowledgeable* people did she suffer, and wasn't it worse for her that her spirit was so strong? You see, a lesser spirit would have acquiesced, but no—a fiercely independent spirit, whoever they are, mentally wounded or not, will fight back. And fight back. Fight to the end. What an uneven contest she had. Do you remember them telling her to back up into the cell when she was tethered by rope, and hooded, and shackled?

Was she the scapegoat that should end our need for scapegoats? Unfortunately that will not happen.

I mention her briefly because I have been caught in the middle of all or part of this, most of my life. Arrogance matched with ignorance and intelligence without compassion are the two forms of individual despotism. For years the idea that I would bring up a book I had read to certain friends meant I was pretending to be superior, and it would hurt their feelings, for as mechanics or journeymen they had no time for books. So I then went to certain university settings, where those with less than a doctorate, or a rather pedestrian understanding of wine and cheese, and a facile devotion to leftist principles, a glib acceptance of diversity without ever themselves being diverse, were considered less than others.

However, both of these camps can at times exhibit the same tendencies, of schooled arrogance, assumption and ignorance. The boy who tried to light a book I was reading on fire as a joke is one example. The professor stodged full of books who would not stand up for a friend in his department for fear of standing alone is another. One was narrow-minded enough to think I believed education made the man, and he would have none of it. While the professor was a clear example that education does not make the man—the soul does.

So now I must talk about a time gone by.

Long ago, as my father walked back and forth to school, he was bullied, because his mother was considered rich and, too, because she was an outcast—which made the idea of his being persecuted a wholly natural one. And I say "natural" in this way: that it would be only the bravest and most independent who would not take up the cause against him. As we know, psychologists are always trying to determine why the world creates misery for those out of step, and yet no one wants us to be in step more than the psychologists themselves.

There is a picture of my father in school where he is the only one dressed in a tie and white shirt. His mother, who had been born and brought up in Injuntown, and had amassed wealth by operating a moving picture theatre in the twenties, was unaware of what animosity she promoted against her children by her sudden wealth. She positioned her son as a scapegoat and target—and her younger children, too; who he would have to turn about and protect. Worse, thinking of herself as having moved up a notch on the social carousel, she did not allow him friends he was naturally inclined to have. Nor was this completely her fault. Many of the families she targeted had initially targeted her, as being a single mother with a business, and therefore terribly disreputable. There is nothing so uncharitable as the pure. And the pure are both *secular* and *religious*, and I see no real distinction in the harm they can unleash.

Since they had belittled her, she would have nothing to do with them, but the price had to be exacted from her son. She was by far too tough for the mothers to ever tackle her, and indifferent to the children. Consequently her son was the chosen sacrifice. I wondered many times if she knew this.

For she might have understood this by the very movies she played at her theatre. So many of these movies—especially the ones the children of that day flocked to, in the thirties and forties, from the cowboys who took on the dandies as much as the First Nations, to the gangsters who had no use for the sophisticates, to the East Side Kids movies starring Leo Gorcey and Huntz Hall, like *Angels with Dirty Faces*—were movies that played to the notion of scapegoat; that is, the rich snots getting what they deserved, because the audience had become emotionally attached to the popular idea of defending their own.

In the audience's mind *their own* were good guys, of course— those who did not read, and had no reason to learn, because they knew already the street, the neighbourhood. They could spot the stranger, the one out of step, a mile down the road.

In the East Side Kids movies that played when my father was a boy, it was diabolically precise—at least concerning his supposed social strata—a rich boy taken care of by a nanny, who for some reason wanders into the turf of the East Siders, who in league with the audience in the theatre would know this boy needed a good comeuppance.

And so the boy is given what he deserves. He is always a weak boy, a nanny's boy, unaware of the ways of the world and the implications of being him. He is left without his money, with a black eye, sitting in his underwear. How hilarious this supposedly is.

Of course the entire set-up is a complete reversal of a heroic stance, but is always fraudulently positioned as such. (There is in these movies a sense of antisemitism here, as well, played out under the cloud of acceptable 1933 European Fascism.)

I take these movies as the template of that which followed for decades, in one way or the other, lying about who the outsider really was, and therefore conforming to a societal ideal that needs sameness and uniformity.

The East Side Kids films and dozens of other movies are actually forever in league with the movie-going public in blind obedience and self-congratulatory conformity to taking on the rich snots, who have gone or go to Ivy League schools. There is a built-in cultural dynamic at play—and it buffers the audience with a coat of armour, as surely as Solomon's shields. It is the idea of being a "regular guy or gal" that cleanses the East Side gang from responsibility no matter how they themselves retaliate against the world, and bully and demean.

The regular guys—and yes, gals—show up everywhere in these movies, and today are seen in dozens of movies each year. Movies that continually tell you how you must act in order to be free. Oh, what I am saying is it plays out day to day, as well, on every school ground and in almost every classroom. *Classifying who is justly a target, and who might target them.*

My father was supposedly not poor—his mother certainly had been. But my father *was* poor. For he was left alone, many days and nights, and protected himself and his brother and sister as best he could. The idea that he had money made him a pariah that is a poverty bred if not born. As long as he lived, he remembered a teacher who was nice to him, kind to him, because almost no one else ever was. He was the solitary rich boy—and they his enemies were, for lack of a better example, *the East Side Kids.*

Still if you watch these movies closely, the poverty that these East Side Kids experience is never alone or lonely. That is, though they are set up as underdogs to the audience, who can sympathize over the injustice perpetrated against them, their experience of being underdog is blessed with the audience's compassion, unlike that of the rich boy. It is understood that there can be no compassion for him.

He in fact is the real scapegoat. The audience as far as I can remember never catches on.

That is, those watching can laugh at his mortification, for they have long ago been taught to conform and, in a way, never to stand alone. To never be a rat. That is the one true secret of their inheritance. They can belong to the real society but only if they obey the tenets of that society. If one of them crossed the floor to offer his hand to the rich boy, it would confuse the movie patrons and cause a moral questioning no one wanted.

For it is the audience who in the end becomes the moral scolds.

"*Ha ha ha*—he got what he deserved." The gloat is Fascistic, of course.

In the way of the street the rich boy is dupe and mark ready to be conned by the *real people*—that is, *the real Americans*.

In fact they are the ones shouting orders at each other, at times loud and boorish, all of which is considered liberated behaviour from the constraints of society.

Yes, I know I have watched a lot of movies from all ages. Nothing shows society less tolerant and more bigoted than this rehearsal of *democratic* value. I suppose one of the movies that elicits this, and exemplifies it as much as any, is the 1944 movie *Laura*, with Clifton Webb, whose character's persona, the prissy intellectual murderer

Waldo Lydecker, heightens our prevalent notion of the cerebral man as being powdered by effeminate and cowardly cunning.

The mob can cheer—and we all do—when he is finally done in and the femme, played by Gene Tierney, is safely in the arms of the rugged detective, played by Dana Andrews. This is American value at its highest mark.

But as Lord Byron expressed it: "I wish men to be free / As much from mobs as from kings." He knew that both have an equal jurisdiction toward malice.

Of course I have found terrible and stringent intellectual malice at university, happy to create the same pestilence for the scapegoat.

The Waldo Lydeckers have their moments, too.

A scapegoat is a good person to torment. Scapegoat coming from the Jewish tradition of the selection of one animal to be slaughtered as tribute for the entire flock.

Most people in our society pick scapegoats. Like I say, my grandmother, scapegoat herself because of being a woman with a business back in the 1920s, should have understood these implications. But she either did not know, or did not believe, it was a serious matter. It was a serious matter to my father.

When he was a child, he was left in the care of nannies who tormented and abused him, for certain private reasons. Beat him and scolded him. One reason being that my grandmother, by then widowed, had married a Protestant and my father was in part English. Which is exactly what the scapegoat in the East Side Kids movies is often portrayed as. Nothing made my father less a part of the small-town values of the time, and the very gregarious values shown on her screen. Movies she travelled to Montreal to buy, in order to play to people who could be reinforced in their dislike of her and my father. A strange transference, you may say. But nonetheless one I myself became aware of before the age of eight.

I really do not think my father ever caught on.

Then when my grandmother decided to remarry, my father was a stark reminder to his Irish stepfather of whom my grandmother had married before. That is, the English pianist. My father was often beaten when his stepfather was drunk, and many times putting his two siblings behind him, my father would try to stave off a beating by holding up a knife. But since he was just a child, there was little hope of it.

"He tried to protect us but was just too little to help us," my uncle, tears in his eyes, told me at my father's funeral. "He never told you, but he was beaten like a dog from the time he was five."

So now you can ask why Ashley Smith—determined to fight to the end—as a Canadian scapegoat is important to me.

Like her, my father had in many respects no one in the world to care for him, and none to care for his brother and sister unless he do so. I am not saying my grandmother did not love them. I am saying, simply speaking, she did not know how to show it. She was long before women thought it fashionable, independent in a way that made her unfashionable.

The tendency to demonstrate willingness to be the same has always been something most of my family fought against. That is the primary source of two things not mutually exclusive: independence and hardship. But my grandmother had no ability to juggle the family at the same time. Nannies were hired, and often the children were left alone with young girls as sure in their ignorance as in their vanity. There was a thrill to belong to those who hated wealth, but worked for a woman who had some; good Catholic girls who would rush to tattle.

So no matter how he aimed to please as a child, he would lose. And his torment was an outing of grievous nature that my grandmother did not see, and could not fathom. Or perhaps she was just too concerned with other matters.

She certainly had other matters to be concerned about. Other businessmen had tried to put her out of business by getting a bank manager to foreclose on her mortgage after her first husband died. That she was able to get a loan from a lumber baron, and repay it, by getting a monopoly on talking pictures, which put her competition out of business, made her a serious target.

They tried to blow her theatre up in 1930 when people were inside. It did not happen because her brother-in-law found the dynamite.

I suppose this is looked upon as fantastic. But not to my family. She became a target, and wealthy and reclusive and bitter. In some ways I can't blame her. But looking closely, I want people to know that my grandmother and my father were looked upon as the *victimizers, not the victims*. With the lie that the incensed mob always uses to pursue the victimizer into the ground. It is a horrible thing to admit that our society still uses scapegoats to call out shame across the aisle against those they target. That pitchforks and torches are still carried in the night against some poor man or woman running away. Our churches might now be empty, gospels laughed at, but the zealots are still here, as many as before. The truth of the first stone that Christ gave us is as true now as it always was.

And when I look back at the portion already written, I understand that my father lived in a world of violence every bit as consuming as some of the boys who lived in dire poverty ever did. So he became what he was: a man alone.

It is all gone now, of course. That generation is dead. The deeds they did are done. The hopes they had are gone. The hilarity of the scapegoat in the end might not have been so hilarious after all. When he turned and fought back one day, he beat three of them silly. They stopped bothering him then. I don't think it was in time.

Yet what I want to talk about, in some small way is the lie.

The lie of the movie hero as scapegoat.

How strange it is that the man alone in our society is often cherished—often after the fact—and that the idea of standing alone is something coveted by those who wish to prove themselves, to say that their lives have meant more because they have struggled that much more against the common physics of the herd.

That is the real secret of those East Side boys—of all those American movies, isn't it—you know, the hero triumphs in the end. John Travolta dresses in leather because he is a rebel; a rebel with a pack of followers always behind him.

The hero and his audience secretly know the dynamite will be found and the crowd will be with him when he rushes the bunker unarmed.

He will not be beaten like a dog by his stepfather without recompense, or choke on the floor like little Ashley Smith being watched by guards who wanted to prove themselves immutable to one another.

You see, I have learned that very often *in real life* the audience is the one to put the dynamite there. And to continue to kick when someone is down in the university common room. To run away and not stand up for a friend. To be the guard smirking behind the glass.

You see, beaten and bound Ashley Smith was the real deal. My beaten and abused father was the real deal.

The real scapegoat—the real deal—is tarred with brush so thick no one would want it. That's the real truth. He/she as scapegoat is alone in satin sheets or not. No one cheers my friend. And often the pain, no matter how one succeeds in life, does not go away.

In so many respects our culture, which relishes individuality, can't stand to be alone, and needs someone who stands alone to hate. The mob crowds together and calls itself "brave." And hate and division mark our society from top to bottom, everyone now is categorized, and make no mistake, all categorizing is used not to celebrate but to damn. Rural men are bigots, learned men are weak. Sometimes, oftentimes, neither is true. Ashley Smith was sad, and hurt and alone, and fought—fought to the end, and there was no help at all. Those who watched her die actually thought they were the ones who were free.

The posture of freedom is not free if it accuses what it does not take the time to understand. And you will always recognize what is posture in the end.

In the movies I refer to, the "supposed" loner always gives himself away by wearing the ducktail, is adorned with the right leather jacket, blessed by the right tokens of rebellion, storming into the office to tell the boss to go to hell, and smirking with his friends just before the final curtain falls.

Oh, but the real scapegoats are unheralded until such time as the mob disperses. They are arrested and tormented for throwing crab-apples on a street, and by the mendacity of justice persecuted unto death. They are beaten and kicked like my father trying to protect his little brother, without a friend in the world to help.

No one wants to be alone, but some of us—well, some of us have to. We have no choice. Alone or die. Strange, I know. I do know. But here's the secret: as long as we've been alive, those who stand alone have never been given the other option.

Christ wanted us to realize few are brave enough to cast the first stone—but anyone and everyone in a mob of "regular gals and guys" will freely cast the second.

2011–2015

HUNTING

THOUGH I BELIEVE THAT IF SOMEONE EATS MEAT, THEY SHOULD be morally obligated to kill at least once in their lifetime that which they eat, I have not hunted seriously since 1995. That year I hunted in the south of the province above the granite rocks of the Fundy coast and I hunted until later in November. It was cold weather that autumn, with snow mixed with rain along the coast during the day, and deer would make their way along the trails and down to the rocky beach for salt, and I hunted in among those deer trails intersecting one another. Here in spruce and birch cover the brooks flowed to the bay, and old logging roads, forgotten for half a century or more, allowed for deer to travel unseen and unmolested to the shore at ebb tide and back up to the hills in the evening time, to lie in the long grass unseen in wood thicket.

There was an apple orchard, too, where I hunted, and on the first day I made it to the orchard at dawn and then moved along a deer trail that ran diagonally from that old logging road to the quiet brook that swept under windfalls and there I stayed for most of the morning. I had the ability then to find a place where deer moved during the rut, where the buck would paw the ground and mark his territory, and where he would circle around to see if a doe had entered the area. I hunted alone, from the time I was twenty-three years of age, and I would sit as quietly as possible for hours on end. There were many deer in the south of the province that year, though they were generally not as large as those in the north of the province, and I was sitting in a forgotten part of the world, too, near three or four moss-ravaged tombstones, the resting place of a mother and her five children who had died in 1851. The village they once belonged to having nothing to mark it except those forlorn graves.

Now and again along those old trails I would catch sight of a coyote slinking on its belly, or watch an osprey in the low, darkening clouds. And it was cold that first day, too, and threatened snow. So I knew snow would come either this day or the next, and the cold would make the deer move.

I had with me a knapsack, with a Thermos of tea, a lunch, a small skinning knife and some chewing tobacco. And I had a chew of tobacco and a cup of tea about ten that morning, and listened to the soundlessness of the woods and the shrill, lowly caw of a crow as it flew from nowhere into nowhere, and I thought of that woman and her children, and how they left Ireland long, long ago, with such hope, and how their very resting place was a part of a community that no longer even existed, known only to a coy dog or hunter or a lonely passerby.

———

I used a British .303 rifle with a Tasco scope, set at the lowest range for I was in close quarters, and I was using 180-grain bullets: that is, bullets with medium hitting power for deer. But I have used this bullet for moose, as well, to good effect. I had a clip with five bullets, with one in the chamber, six bullets in all, and I never had any more bullets on me, and never felt I needed more. For a long time, when I was younger —that is, younger than I was in 1995—I never used a scope, either, but over time I had long shots at both moose and deer and felt a scope necessary. After a while, as the day stilled and it got later, I took a walk out across the logging road to the apple orchard and stayed there. Then as the daylight reflecting in my scope dimmed almost to nothing, I took my clip out of the rifle and headed back to my truck in the dark.

The next morning I got to the apple orchard at dawn, and took a walk down the logging road to the beach. On the logging road, about five hundred yards from the deer trail where I was sitting the previous day, a large buck had pawed the gravel over, and a little farther down there were the criss-crossed claws of a bear paw, where a male bear not yet gone to den had meandered up the road the night before and into the orchard. Knowing this a person should be careful when coming into or leaving an orchard, for though a spring bear is particularly cranky, an autumn bear can be, as well, and not too many people I know want to shoot one. I know I don't. But bears range far and wide here, and do number in the thousands. So rural people in closer proximity worry about them, especially if they have small children.

The deer population is healthy here, too, and that day it was turning bitter and I knew soon it would snow. I made my way back into the spruce and birch cover, along the deer trail that ran above a fertile

stream down to the hidden brook, and waited. There was ice form-
ing along the trail and in the stream itself, and the wind had picked
up, as it often did after mid-morning, and by one in the afternoon
the snow began to fall. Oh, at first lightly enough, but soon it began
to fall so hard it was difficult to see. So I continually checked my
scope cover for two reasons: one to see if it was actually protecting
the scope itself, to keep the lens from fogging; and two, to see if it
would flip off easily if I did get a chance to take a shot at a deer.

Here I had time to think, and listen to the rumbling of the tractor
trailers off to the north carrying tons of wood away to be processed,
either for wrapping paper, newsprint or toilet paper, the great roads
they were on hidden in our wilderness and running throughout
the province, and I realized that the great devastation done to our
land is almost never done for the benefit of rural people, but done to
fulfill an urban need. It is a subtle understanding that comes when
one witnesses the hundreds and thousands of acres thrashed up and
torn away, so we can read books and newspapers telling us to be
conscientious about the environment. That is, we can pay much lip
service to much we do not understand.

   As the snow fell, it began to cover up those old tombstones for
the 144th time, and by two in the afternoon my feet and my hands
were freezing and my tea was cold. But here is what I believe—and I
am asking no one else to agree: that hunting has as much to do with
determination and resolve as anything else. And one should not be
allowed to be comfortable while they kill. That is, I was resolved then
to hunt, and now I am not.

——

I have known men who do not hunt and respect them a good deal, and I know a man who hunted once and did not again—another who had the rifle aimed and could not fire at the little partridge he had in his sights. I knew people who lived in a farm down the road from us. Each fall when they killed a pig the boy would go for a walk and not return until after dark, while the girls would go to their bedroom and lie on the bed with pillows over their ears. And who can blame them. For it might be a lesson to us who do eat meat, that the killing of a pig is at times more gruesome and cruel than the killing of a whitetail deer, or a moose. It is something we should know or at least have some understanding about.

And the amount of meat you get is about the same.

I watched as the day grew dark and then stilled. Then, everything stopped—as if the heart rate of the world lowered. Most people who spend time in the woods understand this and realize this is when the deer begin to move along their rut marks. From an hour before dark until it was too late to see is perhaps the best time for hunting. Still, the snowfall was great and had covered up the blond, deadened grasses, and wisped off the branches of the gnarled spruce in front of me. I was thinking that the male bear whose tracks I saw had by now gone to den, and realized that it was about 4:20—and that I had a long walk back in the snow, along a faded logging road. And then a long drive home that evening.

I was kneeling on one knee, thinking of picking up my knapsack, when I heard a slight noise. I couldn't see anything—but I did know there was a deer there. I took the safety off my rifle. Took a deep breath, waiting ten seconds. I heard another twig move. Then a loud snap.

I released my scope cover, but when I did, the elastic string vibrated. There was utter silence for a long moment.

I knew the deer had stopped, and was listening. So I knew, too, I had no time to wait. I stood and fired. The deer turned too late, a patch of snow jolting off its back. I ejected the shell, put another in the chamber and fired again. The buck stumbled, tried valiantly to stand, fell sideways, sitting up in the snow when it died. It was an eight-point buck—probably the one that had pawed the gravel yesterday. One of his tines had been broken in a rut fight. He died in the only world he had ever known or understood.

It was the last year I ever hunted. I moved to Toronto, where I lived for thirteen years.

There at times in posh restaurants, elk or caribou or venison would be on the menu for $29.95. On occasion I would see a coyote skirting the traffic. I would read newspapers printed on paper harvested from home. And at times I would think of the young buck with the broken tine, and realize I would probably never hunt again.

Once an urban boy asked, "What is it like to kill things?"

Well, son, something a lot like that.

EAST OF EDEN

THE MIRAMICHI REGION OF NEW BRUNSWICK—HOME TO ONE OF
the grandest rivers on the planet, the true home of the great Atlantic
salmon, the Cunard Line and the man who financed the Spitfire—
has come under attack once again by a national reporter, who
whined that we did not come up to her expectations: we were a
backward place.

The superiority others feel toward someone is insidiously transparent to those who suffer the assault, and Maritimers have suffered
from this endlessly over the last century.

Here are some examples of the gaiety of dismissal I have come
across:

An economics professor from the University of Calgary, who sat
beside me during a flight from Calgary to Toronto, asked if I could
fly to the Maritimes from Toronto, or would I transfer to bus or train.

"Dogsled, sir," I said. "Then oxen, and of course my mule."

I'm not sure he got the joke.

A professor from the University of Ottawa was outraged that then New Brunswick premier Frank McKenna arrived at a first ministers meeting in a limo. Hidden behind his concern for the supposed desperate poverty of our province was an elitism, masked as social conscience, that McKenna dare arrive in the same fashion as the professor's Ontario premier. The idea that I moved to Toronto incensed this man, as well, because I had no right to try and be like my betters.

My wife, Peg, after we moved to Ontario, telephoned the Ministry of Health. When she gave her last address as "Saint John, New Brunswick," the woman said, "No, ma'am, I mean your last address in Canada."

Often when we—and I say "we" because it is the place where I was born and raised—come under attack from outsiders, the response has been, naively, to assume that with good publicity or a better media rapport we can change this person's opinion. It was once suggested that if I stopped writing terrible things about the people there, our tourism would improve. I do not write terrible things (or not many), and a tourist's opinions of a place are rarely informed by the kind of literature I write.

But the real problem has nothing at all to do with the Miramichi or the Maritimes: it has to do with the kind of person writing the article that criticizes the Maritimes. None should mind being ridiculed by the foolish, the foppish or the insincere. Nor should anyone assume it a victory to gain their approval.

Why bother informing her who we are? Why wish for her smile as a validation of our worth? Who in God's name is so unconscious of their own worth as a people, as a people on one of the great rivers of the world, that they would ever think they have to list the creature comforts or the silly spectacles, so those who have always viewed us and our ancestors in ignorance will favour us now?

It is not up to us to change anyone's mind; it is up to them. We may convince them for a while, but their salute will fade as soon as our contrived regard does, and she or he or whoever will go back to assuming themselves superior to us once more, and bashing us when possible.

For this kind of assault on our home is a reaction of insecure and provincial people, who can be found in Toronto, as well as anywhere else. I have met many from Ontario who do have more than a passing understanding of their country, but Toronto seems to be a state unto itself.

The people on the Miramichi whom I respect the most would never bother answering this chatter. But it raises the ire of those Miramichiers who believe they belong to the pan-Canadianism expressed by the surface attention of certain programs of CBC Radio. Like their counterparts in Whitehorse, Regina or elsewhere, these Miramichiers have bought into a centralist affectation: that the CBC flings us together and shows us all to be the same. (Gzowski was famous at this, and I believe he meant well without realizing he was condescending.)

Those on my river who treasure the folksy banalities that these programs safely allow are the first to react when pricked. They herd together on radio airwaves across the nation and become the spokespeople for their area, their town or small city, because they cherish someone else's patronizing look at who they are, and believe they have arrived because of it. They'd wear the funniest hat in the parade, pick the banjo and assume the posture, then wait for the same kind of applause given to someone in Saskatoon.

It is easy, then, to see how some consider that they have every right to belong in the way they have been gulled into believing they do—the all-inclusive way. When, once again, by a report in a national newspaper, they are slapped into the realization that our very history makes us targets, they decry the injustice.

My God, boys, I know it's unjust, but why start there? And what does it matter if some reporter filled with the idea of her own entitlement finds you a convenient scapegoat?

Once outside Canada, no one knows Ontario any more than they know New Brunswick, and the world has heard of Kosovo more often than both. When I taught in Virginia, Canada was a red blur to the students there. One told me she thought her father owned an island somewhere near Toronto and asked me if that was where the Miramichi was. Being polite, I said, "Sure." One should not be upset, for I have faced questions as silly from economics professors from Calgary.

So enjoy your Miramichi, boys and girls, this summer and forever. There's not one like it up here.

1999

LAND

THE HOUSE WAS OWNED BY MY FRIEND'S UNCLE—A WHITE
house with a small, enclosed veranda, where a faded, flowered swing
listed to the southwest, while autumn sun glinted on six window-
panes. The uncle used to drink Napoleon wine there on sunny days,
watching the bird feeders he had placed on the maple trees, and
sometimes picking off the squirrels if too many of them started
chasing away the birds.

A host of crab trees, gnarled from the roots up, grew haphazardly in the back, in a field of yellow grass, where the deer came
out. At the end of this field sat a barn with a sagging roof, where
a horse of little worth had lived out its life. Uncle Tate, a widower,
fed it and kept it warm, but used it for nothing and cursed it in
the pasture.

A veteran of the Second World War, he died in 1963, cutting a
new road through for the Fraser lumber mill. I remember Alden
Nowlan's answer to "A little hard work never killed anyone":

"My God—hard work kills people all the time."

It is what those who have not worked, or known those who have, have forgotten.

There was no one to take his house. A distant cousin said it was his. A sister of that cousin said it was hers. I forget how things finally transpired; land was argued over (winter trees frigid under the moon, and everyone arguing over whose moon it was).

Finally, his nephews went into the house and closed it up. What was valued was siphoned off. As teens we passed it a number of times going into the future. The nineteen-foot dory that Uncle Tate had used for herring was left at night against the barn, the pathway he took to the icefield to lay out smelt nets no longer in evidence.

The Beatles came. Everyone was in love. Vietnam and love.

Neil Young sang about a town in North Ontario. Suddenly half my generation wanted to be old—or from a previous generation—a generation that did things by hand, and by rote; a generation that lived off the land, never knowing that even the First Nations themselves wanted at least in part to escape from this. Those who had never mashed more than potatoes were talking to me about milling flour. To dispossessed youth in the cities, it was a great and risky adventure—going off to the boonies, some with their daddy's credit card, and without his blessing. Here in northern New Brunswick was one place those who wanted to change their lives came to.

So in 1972, a new Walden was to be shaped out of Uncle Tate's farmyard, his fourteen acres that bordered the bay, where the wind was so cold even by late August it could chill your blood.

The group was made up mostly of expatriate Americans, and some Canadians, and one or two from New Brunswick. One of Uncle Tate's nephews had left the farm; no longer respecting his loved ones who had shovelled shit to keep him alive, he reached out to gurus who knew far less than his father, and joined the very farm Uncle Tate had worked a little over a decade before.

Her name was Stevie—she was nineteen, wore granny glasses and knitted in Uncle Tate's kitchen as the sunlight glanced over the chimes. She was from Toronto, and the fellow, her mentor, and the mentor of the group, Darren, came from New York. I have a memory of him looking like Jesus, leaning against Uncle Tate's sink and pouring water out, as if at a baptismal:

"Man, you guys don't know what you got here—so you'd better take care of it," he said, pouring out a cup of clear well water. That is, he ordered me to take care of something his own urban culture had reduced to nothing.

"We got a lot a winter," I said.

"That's cool," he said. "That's cool—just get yerself an old lady and tuck in."

"What was your uncle like?" Stevie asked my friend. "Was he a fine man?"

My friend turned beet red.

"He was a sawed-off five-foot-five-inch redneck," my friend said, "who got into fights."

They both laughed, and he looked pleased.

"He was a fine man," I whispered in apology, not to them—but to Uncle Tate for the utter weakness of his nephew.

Tate was a fine man. But not the way they were thinking. When he came back to New Brunswick from the Second World War, he was as wild as a buck and as rough as a night in jail. Peace and love he had in abundance, but not the kind to suffer fools. He'd walk across the river in late March, with the ice breaking around his boots, to get to a dance. That was faith. He was completely colour-blind; he'd love and hate indiscriminately. He got into a fight with the doctor and was in jail when his wife died alone. He never forgave himself that.

By the questions they asked about his life I knew they were hoping for a working-class hero, not hoping for a man but someone they had seen in some movie. And his nephew from rural New Brunswick was so ashamed of his heritage he wanted to belittle it in front of his betters so he could belong—belong to those who wanted to churn butter to prove they were morally superior to a man now dead, who at five-foot-five was as strong as a bull.

I don't think I ever cared for his nephew after this day.

I discovered from this nephew that the newcomers had not come here to learn from the whites, anyway; they did not want what the Uncle Tates knew but to study the First Nations, to learn from them. There would be no going back to what they had all come from. But the First Nations by now owned cars, high-powered boats, TVs and Ski-Doos. And they didn't want to go back, either.

"No, there is no going back for them," my friend said happily. "They are committed to here—this place will be their roots."

"Well, then they will need three hundred years," I said.

The older man in the group, Darren, worried about the First Nations people here.

"We've destroyed them," he said.

"Not entirely," I said (not in defence of us but in defence of them—but he did not get this subtlety).

"It's terrible the way they are treated," he continued. "The Aboriginals are caretakers of our earth—aren't they?"

No one could say Darren was wrong about the first part of the statement. I think he was scolding us with the second. Well, who in North America doesn't deserve to be scolded, more than once, about the First Nations people?

I began to realize that Darren believed in his ability not so much to belong with the First Nations, who would allow him the benefit of vicarious suffering, but to escape who he was, a white, urban, university-educated man in a denim suit, with long hair and love beads. And Tate's nephew gave up his own hard-earned, blow-by-blow knowledge of life here for a notional knowledge in order to belong to a group he considered superior to those people who had already fashioned a complete life out of the soil.

In a certain respect, he was like the First Nations people who were to give up their own knowledge of life and land because the new white settlers had told them to. Soon they were going to make a canoe of bark, fish in the traditional way, plant under the June moon—they had a pocketful of seeds. Pocketful of dreams.

They spent October in the yellow trees, cutting and limbing the wood they were to burn, but didn't get it yarded until late and then left it where it was until well after the first storm. After a time they reminded me of a little band of orphans, nowhere much to go. Stevie's cheeks were often streaked with red, as if she had just cried. I wondered where she had come from. But she was here now and under orders from a guru who probably gave orders as relentlessly as any daddy she had run from. I saw her trying to carry wood to the house and stumbling under the weight, as if she were carrying a cross she could neither bear nor understand. It might have been like forcing an Indian woman to go to church in the eighteenth century. The feeling of being displaced must have been almost as great.

But she continued to carry her wood.

Watching her in those days, I thought of a thousand women who had done the same a century before—of my mother-in-law, left a widow with nine children at the age of forty-two, a country girl—of my mother, who grew up in the heart of what any one of these people would consider the wilderness and did housework from the time she was four. Of my uncle, who, at thirteen, was sent through the woods to find my grandfather, while my grandmother, holding a double-barrelled shotgun, held off a group who was trying to take the property. She would have shot them if she had had to. For her to wax eloquent about the danger of guns and the need to take safety courses was not an option at that moment. Or of my paternal grandmother, who knocked a cow cold with one punch (a feat not to be equalled by any literary figure in Canada, save Malcolm Lowry).

When it became very cold, Stevie would sit in our corner store for hours, pretending to do crossword puzzles in the daily newspapers. She was hiding from the guru, who intimidated her and intellectually bullied her.

I often saw a look of dull confusion, as if she were a lost Girl Guide. In a way her plight was a lesson to me about the First Nations, about how their lives were so finally and tragically changed after 1605. Stevie suddenly brought that home, without her ever knowing it. And where, I thought, could she ever go now? Nowhere. Not with winter setting in and no tickets home. There was a hush over the land that they had rented, and frost clung to the turned-down and twisted grasses; their wood lay yarded as haphazardly as fallen soldiers. There was no way to dispel the cold and no way to get rid of the smoke from their damp maple and birch. No way to make the light stay when it was getting dark, no way to make the chickens look happy, no way to make the barn stand straight again. No one had money for those things. And night—night came at six, at five, at four-thirty.

The locals became interested in helping out. For no better reason (and a damn good reason it was) than these were people and it was Christmas. And many of my friends who were their age dropped in on them with presents.

They brought deer meat and homemade wine, fresh-grown grass, and other forms of libation. But it became a strange celebration. It reminded me of Tolstoy's quip that at least as much is known in the country as the city, and probably more.

When Darren spoke to us of wanting to build a geodesic dome, he was very surprised to find out that our friend had quit school in grade ten and had built the first dome in New Brunswick, drawing on his own plans and intelligence, and reading Buckminster Fuller.

When Darren said he would fish for his food, it was another friend who brought them ten smoked salmon. This was not one-upmanship. The little town was just the land extended. Until I was twenty-four, I could carry my rifle from my house into the woods for a deer hunt. It is not that Darren did not know the land—he did not know himself, and the land simply told him this. Sooner or later the land does. I know he wanted to live in harmony like the first people and wanted the First Nations people to be his champions of the forest and his protectors of the environment. But that said only one thing: he had never allowed them an option; in his life he never really looked upon them the way they should have been looked upon from the first: as men.

Life went on. There were chores to be done, by people who had never done chores before. They spoke of sharing, but it was contractual, not emotional. It seemed to me there was more love in the place when Uncle Tate lived alone and fired off his shotgun at his visitors as a joke.

By January there were dissenters. That month a young man got a job in town. Another went away—and then another. Tate's nephew left in a dispute over something.

I met Stevie coming out along the back road one day. She was carrying a saucepan, with nothing in it. Someone had told her there were winter berries to collect, but she had found none, for there were none. We stood and talked for a moment in the freezing gale of late afternoon.

"We are going to have a really fine farm," she told me.

I knew that was nonsense. But I was so sorry for her at that moment. She had come to womanhood in what kind of city, to feel so left out, like so many of my generation? Cast out, of something. I'm not even sure what anymore. All she had known was concrete. Why had this happened? What sad turning away from her family did she have, in what hot, vacant urban apartment or house tucked between two asphalt roads? An argument over the war—or a parent trying too hard to buy her love, or loving her too little? Did they even know where she was anymore? She was still a child, really.

"So you aren't going home?" I said.

"Oh—no—no," she said, and smiled. "I'll never go."

It was a victory for her to say this. I might have told her that I knew a family who arrived at this little place she was now in 1840—and lived their first winter in a cave about a mile from where we were talking, losing three children. I might have told her my relatives came over after the Battle of Culloden, and one walked from Pennsylvania in 1805 and settled upon the Northwest. To keep her chin up.

I discovered at that moment that there is something about the land—you look unnatural on it if you are unnatural; you look greedy upon it if you are, lazy if you tend to be. If you are frightened of guns or wildlife, the land will inform you. Nervous on the water? The water will let you know. There is no escaping who you are once you are here, on the Miramichi—or anywhere else, for that matter. It is what the First Nations saw of us—it is what I saw of her; she with the saucepan with nothing in it.

The man Darren who made the rules was simply selfish—and in a sense, beyond all his ethical talk of First Nations, a prude. This is what the land said he was. And the land does not lie.

In late January one of them went and got a job. He worked at a garage in Barryville, repairing snowmobiles, and would come home every night late. He supported this little family of outcasts by doing a job hundreds of men did without complaint simply because life required that he do it. And it was he who got to meet the First Nations on even terms, because he worked alongside the Micmac man, Jacob Paul, who co-owned the garage that repaired small engines.

Then he found a girl in Neguac and moved out.

So there was only Stevie and her mentor, Darren, left. They were the last. And in that winter, living alone, they found the dream had somehow disappeared. But what dream was it? I don't think any of them, including Darren, really knew.

Still, in some way, it must have been a noble dream, a kind of idealism that can only be hatched in torment, from a society writhing in pain. The looking for a better world, in Uncle Tate's few acres at the edge of the earth. A little society in the wilderness, born in the city, believing animals were Bambis and berries were for the taking, flying back home on a jet plane where if lucky they could still believe those things. They found here only the pain they believed they had left behind, and in the end blamed us because we had no balm or magic to help them relinquish this pain. The simple pain of being women and men, no matter what land you stood on and of what race you were.

Darren left one afternoon, saying he would be back—that he was going into town for supplies. His poncho on a hook in the corner near his leather hat assured Stevie of his return. But he did not come back. She waited by the window, his supper in the warming oven. He became safe again, when being unsafe was no longer a game.

Stevie stayed by herself, looking out those porch windows, waiting for her friend. She made it until March. Sometime about Saint Patrick's Day I saw her doing her crossword in the corner store. There was a storm outside and everything in the world was white.

She was happy, she said; the wood was drier, and people had made her welcome. She was working two nights a week in this store, selling cigarettes and Tampax. But she needed to take a course, she thought—and come back next year. Next year would be better. The terrible things in the world would be gone. She would get a horse, maybe one of those Morgans. Suddenly she reached up and kissed my forehead and squeezed my hand. She walked on and I watched her go out of my life. It's been almost forty years. The house is gone, and no one waits, and none of them have ever been back. They didn't have much luck. For a while many of us might have believed a new world would come. Perhaps that's what we've all been watching for, whenever we look up at the sky.

I walked beyond Uncle Tate's land last autumn. There had been two days of snow. I walked toward the hundredth new chop-down that had come since the mill started its new process. I carried my little .32 Winchester—but I have not fired a rifle at game in years. I trick myself into hunting by not hunting now. Usually I find a tin can to fire at, sight the rifle in, for next year.

My family—here for over two and a half centuries—is gone from the river, and in the summer the brooks babble to tell me so. My mother died in 1978, my father died ten years ago, and all the children have left. We have gone away, but we do come back. In a sense, once a part of the land, we can never leave. We didn't become peace lovers, but we do love, fiercely, I suppose.

There is no town here now. A city sprawls with lights toward its destiny. The trees are muted and thrashed, as pockets of the forest no longer exist at all.

I walked toward the high ground beyond his house, next to the power lines. The ground was dug up that day with fresh tracks and scrapes. In one of those tricks of fate I saw the old saucepan Stevie had used to collect her winter berries. It had been tossed up out of the dirt that had buried it for years. I wondered how her life had gone, and if she had ever found the place she wanted.

Then turning toward the chop, I saw a little doe. As I approached, she made a heroic attempt to stand. Her left hind leg was caught in a coyote snare, and she was hunkered down beneath the snow and thrashed trees. All around and everywhere I looked the snow and earth had been torn up, where a gigantic battle had raged above Uncle Tate's old farmyard. The night before, the buck had stayed to protect the doe in the snare from the coyotes. And he must have fought like hell. The coyotes—here almost as big as wolves—hadn't been able to get to her. I do not know if the buck lived, but he had done the job given him. Like Uncle Tate with his wife, he didn't know why she was caught up. The world had betrayed them both: the snare cynically said neither of them mattered. Still the buck had fought like a bastard. Never left his poncho on a nail.

I managed to cut the snare. She stood and bolted, cracking the limbs of some birch trees, and was gone, into what was left of a world that didn't exist any longer.

I SUPPOSE I COULD SPEAK
OF BEAUTY

(Talk delivered to Atlantic School of Theology graduates, 2010)

I SUPPOSE I COULD SPEAK OF BEAUTY IN THE WAY MANY PEOPLE must think of it—pretty pictures of streams or delicate flowers in some forgotten place; and I suppose I would be right except for perhaps a blush or two of sadness that we might recall in those places and pictures of streams, and parts of our youth now gone that we can never recapture—and in that sadness we might see beauty, too, and a longing for things that can never come back, like a childhood fled away, over the sad, longing dunes of our past.

It imparts wisdom, this beauty—finally it must, for it makes us reflect on the idea—the one idea that in the four corners of the world, and in all the places we have ever been, no matter how we look at it, and how mankind has bled it away, beauty will and will forever remain, soluble and indivisible from something greater, some unquestionable desire to know what is in fact true. "Truth is beauty," Keats does say. For strange as it may seem, there is no everlasting beauty without man or woman to be witnesses to it, and man or woman searches for the truth of beauty throughout their lives. That is the secret: we long for and search for beauty, even if we are to find it, as Tolstoy says in a puddle of dirt that briefly reflects the sky.

And sometimes that is all we have to see—sometimes that is all we have to hold to, amid the sordid squalor that comes to us, from one report or another. Because the sky reflected in the puddle is Tolstoy's way of imploring us to realize the gifts of man's greater soul.

So then I am not certain if there is anything else man searches for but beauty. And if that is the case, then we must search well for it, and must look hard to find it, and must seek it where it rightly is, and not be seduced by what it pretends to be. That is the secret, also, the secret of beauty, that I will speak about briefly—for I do not need to go on so long about it—for true beauty has in its own way a finality, and a truth, and it must have, for it is, this true beauty, always at war with that which must try to destroy it.

And what tries to destroy it? What attempts to destroy it is the false beauty that parades as beauty, that sets itself up in glory, and parades and postures and struts and makes us want what it is, and if we want what it is bad enough, if we need what it is, we must in some respects kill the beauty that God always intended for us.

This, then, is the dilemma cast and wrought out in our human souls.

So there is a difference between these two beauties, and this difference is profound and earth shaking and I might even say—in fact, I have to say—apocalyptic.

Yes, the war against these two beauties is apocalyptic.

But we have seen it this war—in Homer's *Iliad*, in Virgil, in Dante,

Shakespeare and Milton, too; in Emily Brontë and Emily Dickinson, in Malcolm Lowry—in all the writers who have transposed into their work the longing for truth against the odds. This fight for beauty was shown to us in the work of all the prophets.

And of course, by Christ himself.

This line—"beauty will save the world"—comes to us from Fyodor Dostoyevsky, and we must recognize what he meant by this, this frightened, brave, incorrigible man, who lived and died well over a century ago.

We must reflect on this idea that beauty will save the world, for it is a great and harsh and wondrous claim.

And if we visit his books, we might begin to see what he means— not for his books or Russia alone but for all mankind. And we might realize that it in fact is a fight for the very essence of life.

In one of the greatest scenes in *The Brothers Karamazov*, Dmitri and Alyosha are in the garden at the back of their small town, talking about Dmitri's proposal of love to the beautiful Katerina and the allure of the also beautiful, earthly Grushenka, when he suddenly makes this profound statement:

"The devil and Christ fight for the souls of the men of the earth, and the weapon they use is beauty."

And we think: How could the devil and Christ use the same weapon? Well, reflecting upon it, they both use beauty as the weapon, but the weapon of beauty is so profoundly different. One in fact is the anathema of the other.

I would like us to reflect briefly on Dmitri's statement that Christ and the devil fight for the souls of men and the weapon they use is beauty.

Later in one of the most famous chapters of all literature, called "The Grand Inquisitor," their brother Ivan speaks about Torquemada, whose blood lust perverted Christianity and Catholicism.

Ivan, using the Grand Inquisitor's logic, condemns Christ. Citing Satan's three temptations in the desert, he decries that Christ could have helped the world by accepting the devil's offer. It would have been so simple and needed—and Christ at that moment in the desert could have so suddenly done what man wanted him to do for over two thousand years: rule the world with his love!

So Ivan's question becomes the Grand Inquisitor's: Why didn't he? Why did he not accept the empires of the world as his own—for accepting it would have brought all the souls to him, and would not then he have been able to create heaven on earth? And that he did not create it made him lose it—and so, Ivan says, the Grand Inquisitor is now obligated to burn Christ at the stake, to prevent the perversion of a Christianity the Inquisitor believes in. And it is Christ's fault, he says, that this has happened.

The one problem is—and we see it, in the smile of pride, and in the arrogance in the questions—that the Inquisitor has accepted the world, has embraced its empire and, in some grave way, has demonstrated how he in accepting the world perverted the very beauty Christian men and women are asked, and demanded, to seek.

And this is what Christ knew when he said, "Do not tempt the lord thy God."

For great as empires are, this is not the beauty Christ wishes us to embrace.

So Christ could no more embrace the devil's beauty than he could succumb to Satan's entreaty. That is, the nature of the beauty Christ offers and the beauty the earth offers is fundamentally different—

and it is this difference that every poet and scribe who ever wrote has tried to delineate for themselves as well as others. There is a secretive, otherworldly beauty—a beauty that exists on a different plane, within the realm of empathy—the beauty that transgresses against helplessness and hopes to alleviate pain that illuminates the beauty Christ fights with—this is the message of the conversation in the garden between Dmitri and Alyosha. The beauty of Christ is a beauty that understands man's nature of helplessness and hopes to alleviate it against all the odds the world has thrown up —against the profusion of cant, and pride and scorn set against this helplessness. Christ's beauty reminds us to set out to deploy what Shakespeare deploys, the fact that "They laugh at scars who never had a wound."

The Grand Inquisitor laughs at scars, delights in fact in wounds.

In fact the temptation in the desert is in the final analysis what has happened to our Grand Inquisitor. He has succumbed to such a beauty as the tempter offered. It is as beautiful and unblemished as a statue of some Greek god in the sun. And it wrought him nothing in the end but false piety and false treasure and—in the beauty of his auto-da-fé—hell.

Christ's answer to why he cannot give himself into Satan's temptation is in fact in the very persona of Torquemada himself.

But do these things, the temptation and the inquisition, show up in modern day, or are they so anachronistic they are not worthy to speak about? People in fact refrain from speaking about them as if to recoil from a hot stove. As if they did not matter—or more to the point (for if they did not matter, no one would recoil so quickly) that they do matter so much we become embarrassed by their presence, and do not know how to relate our idea of them.

But no matter what age, this argument does manifest itself.

When Mr. Wilberforce the slave trader embraced the money and emblazoned the beauty of the slave trade—to deliver healthy, beautiful bodies of girls and boys, men and women for profit across the sea—it was not so long ago. And when he was in a ravaged storm in the Atlantic and begged Christ if there was Christ to save him, saying he would not trade in beautiful bodies anymore, that was not so long ago. And when the storm calmed, he let his cargo of frightened human beings free, and years later, finally free himself from what he had partaken in, in youth, he wrote for us the song all of us have heard, "Amazing Grace."

And that was not so long ago.

In 1938 Prime Minister Chamberlain and his entourage invited to Dresden (the second meeting with Hitler)—during the Munich crisis over Czechoslovakia—was overcome by German beauty—in fact he was seduced by beauty: There were thousands of Nazi flags waving in the sun, the lake was crystal blue, the great suites in the grand hotel were plush with carpet and every whim of food and beverage an Englishman might desire. And the SS guards, young and handsome, tall and strong, stood guard, in black helmets and white gloves, with their bayonets glinting. While little blue-eyed, blond girls and boys dressed in traditional dresses and trousers, their faces glowing with health, handed out flowers and plums and oranges to the guests.

Yes, this was the paradigm of beauty, and it was remarked by everyone in the world as beauty—by the Paris and London papers as beauty—by our own Lord Beaverbrook, as well.

Beauty that the world wanted and needed. And because of this beauty, the beauty that Hitler presented to his guests, Czechoslovakia was dismantled, and peace assured for all those who needed and longed for beauty. The seduction was in fact the seduction by beauty of something greater than one might first imagine. It was a beauty that took away courage and honour.

As Winston Churchill, one of the few dissenters in all of England, said later to an almost empty House of Commons:

"You were given the choice between war and dishonour. You chose dishonour, and you will have war."

That was a kind of beauty—the kind we seem to be unable to resist—and the kind that allows, sooner or later, disgrace.

But I will now mention the other beauty—the beauty that came from that beauty in order to counter it.

It was in 1941, and the Russian city Leningrad was surrounded, possibly by some of those very same SS troops who were so resplendent in Dresden three years before. The city was being bombed and strafed; people were starving—there was no way into the city of death except by the lake on the eastern shore, Lake Ladoga. And in December of that year a middle-aged truck driver was waiting at the far end of the lake, walking back and forth in the minus-thirty-degree weather, looking anxiously toward the bombed city. He was there for one reason, and for one reason only: he was waiting for the lake to freeze deep enough so he could take a Lorrie across it. And though everyone told him not to risk it, that the ice was not thick enough, he dove his Lorrie onto the windswept ice and, battered by cold and shells from the German guns, made it into the city of death and starvation and despair, with his cargo. He managed to make it against all the odds thrust upon him, in the dark cold and terrified night. He made it.

And his cargo, well then, his cargo—oranges for the children for Christmas.

That simply told is true beauty. It is a beauty that does not seduce but asks us to emulate, a beauty that does not contrive to give but asks us to sacrifice. A beauty that depends and even seems to ask for too much. A beauty that Satan in tempting Christ has no answer for and does not know.

But in the eternal spark of human creation, we know.

A beauty that, Dostoyevsky reminds us, will not destroy, manipulate and seduce, but will save the world.

It follows the firemen up the towers on that dreadful day and watches over a small boat when it turns back into a storm toward a doomed vessel floundering in the swell.

It is in fact the harshest and most necessary beauty the world has ever known. It is the beauty I ask, for all of you graduating this year. It is that beauty that I hope you never relinquish. It is beauty so profoundly startling it is sometimes caught only in a moment among so many other moments in a day.

It is why "Amazing Grace" is sung in death, and the world celebrates with the "Song of Joy" when a man or woman hands over their very last piece of bread.

2009

I WENT DOWN TO MEET
ALDEN NOWLAN

I WENT DOWN TO FREDERICTON TO MEET ALDEN NOWLAN, THE
man from Desolation Creek, Nova Scotia, a founding member of
the Flat Earth Society, whose charter relinquishes Earth to the abyss
somewhere off the farther coast of Newfoundland; member of the
inner court of King James Stewart, the Stewart monarchy in exile
(yes, Stewart—the French changed the spelling to Stuart); honorary
doctor of laws, like one of his heroes, Sam Johnson—both prodigious towering men, with grave knowledge and a curious softheart-
edness, a more curious vulnerability to be a target of their times; like
Sam, as well, a brilliant conversationalist—or more precisely, what
is a Maritime trait, a "monologist"; a cook, and a good one; a secret
watcher of daytime soaps; an intentional lover of bad movies—
which is, to my way of thinking, always a sign of greatness; a self-
taught reader by four years of age, with, by the age of thirty-five, a
library containing thousands of volumes of works on every possible
subject, and thousands of his own poems; a reader of five newspapers a day, who quit school in grade five to work in the woods, which

made him the only poet in the country deemed functionally illiterate by Statistics Canada—a fact he was whimsically proud of; a large, imposing, generous, self-deprecating, hard-drinking, chain-smoking, complex, irascible, irritating wonder of a man, who had been born in poverty, the son of a woodsman and a teenage girl, in the Depression year of 1933 in rural Nova Scotia.

I went down to meet Alden Nowlan, which might have been a title of one of his own poems, and I could quote dozens of them.

I would quote his poems and watch in Sydney, Australia, or Brisbane, or Virginia, or New Orleans, or London, people's faces light up for the first time at the man's genius—recognize themselves in him, and hear in his simple, straightforward words some great eternal wisdom.

It was a wisdom tinged with sorrow, that always came, it seemed, in the form of a parting between friends said at the door on a cold winter evening.

The last time I quoted them (I leave it to others now), people asked about him, at the writers' conference in Brisbane, Australia, in 1993:

"Where is he from?"

"Where can we get his poems?"

"What are the names of his books?"

"Did he win the Nobel Prize?"

One middle-aged woman, whispering in my ear: "His *Cousins*—you know a secret—I grew up like that, here in Australia, that's what I've been trying to say in my work, but I never heard anyone say it like that. Can I write to him? Is he Canadian?"

"He would love you to—and he would answer—but he is gone from us" was the only answer I could give.

He lived at best a precarious childhood, growing up in the Mosherville-Stanley area of central Nova Scotia. There are scenes in the novel about his childhood, *The Wanton Troopers*, that are truly horrific. But as he once said, children can exist in a world adults would go mad in.

By the time Alden Nowlan was thirty-three, he would have the first of his major operations for throat cancer—the doctor telling him that the chances of his living through it were about the same as a Canadian soldier living through the landing at Dieppe in 1942. When the doctor told him he had cancer, he burst out laughing. It seemed so strange. He had gone to see about a sore throat.

He lived through the first operation, and a second one, and a third—losing the muscles in his shoulders as a result—and as a result of that growing a lion-like beard to hide the scars on his throat that his closer friends would sometimes see whenever he sat in his den in his housecoat and leather slippers. He did not quit smoking.

Still, why would he not live through these operations? He had lived through so much before this. Abused as a child of poverty—tormented, abandoned, beaten. Thought of as retarded, and mocked by men and boys he knew, spending years in isolation—discovering mocking came because of their fear of him. He learned over time how prevalent this would be.

Finally he left home at nineteen, never to return, to take a job at the newspaper in Hartland, New Brunswick, the *Observer*, lying about certain qualifications he never had and, as it turned out, never needed. There he formed friendships with people such as Hugh John Fleming and young Richard Hatfield, the latter being a friend he would not desert. In fact, Nowlan would desert so few in his life. Even his father, who treated him cruellest of all, he did not desert.

His poems about and his letters to his father reflect this. In his 1974 novel, *Various Persons Named Kevin O'Brien*, he admitted that he was the only person in the world who ever feared his father, one line that says more about the excruciating circumstances of an impoverished child's life than any report on the subject ever could.

His life as a child, he once said, was the life of Huckleberry Finn—not the romantic freckle-faced kid—that, he said, was Tom Sawyer. No, the world of Huck Finn was both violent and terrifying, and Twain made sure he let us know it was. So, too, did he.

I was on my way to see Alden Nowlan, on my motorcycle on a summer's night, shifting down through the turns on the Killarney Road in Fredericton, during one of the last summers of his life—I did not know this then, of course, though I now suspect he must have. Looking back, he was probably forty-eight years old, so he had done some living. And more than his share of suffering, though he almost never complained and, like James Joyce, had a resolute will to forge out of the smithy of his soul his own destiny. There is something great in that attribute, that rare ability to be one's own man, and to (as Chekhov said) "squeeze the slave from my soul."

Destiny it was. And it was his great intellect, matched with a brave heart, that saw him through. He was a friend of Hatfield and Dalton Camp, of Irving Layton, knew Ernest Buckler, and Pat Lane, and John Newlove; conversed with Morley Callaghan and corresponded with Henry Miller; a friend also of Stompin' Tom Connors; a friend of ordinary men and women everywhere. Sometimes he would pick an area code out of the telephone book late at night and phone the operator in a small town in Virginia or New Mexico to have a chat. Knowing loneliness and human nature, he knew they were often happy to have a person listen to them for a change.

He said he would make a great old man—but he said it the way people do who test the waters, hoping God is listening. At times he matched his age against those whose work he respected, and felt some achievement in outliving them, because death was always so intimate a presence.

He had outlived Keats (and once he smiled and said to me, "Well, except for Thomas Chatterton, who hasn't?"). He had outlived Emily Brontë, Shelley and Byron, and D. H. Lawrence, Dylan Thomas, Brendan Behan and Malcolm Lowry. He was the last to think that earthly longevity was the measure of any man or woman (just look at the names mentioned), but it was no less true that to keep going and keep writing would be fine with him.

Of them all, Keats was his favourite. Not the Keats of school-book misinformation, the wispy English Romantic, but the tough, life-loving, five-foot-four boxer and walker, glorious champion of the underdog, nicknamed "Junkets" by Leigh Hunt, writer of brilliant sonnets and odes who died forsaken by the public an age before. "The magnificent Red-haired Runt" Alden Nowlan called him. Nowlan shared more in common with him than he himself might have thought. Both early on were such bleak prospects and suffered illness, in silence, to almost the same degree.

There is a picture of Nowlan taken when he is about thirteen—a runny nose, a malbuttoned checked woollen bush jacket, a desolate landscape behind him, a lonely gaze out at the camera toward some faraway place. A haunted sadness encompasses everything.

From this picture it would seem amazing to some that he wrote at all—that he wrote poems, astonishing. But that he wrote many of the finest poems ever written by anyone in Canada—a country that in very many ways he loved and in many ways ignored him—miraculous.

His first poems were traditional, but infused with great power and perception. Think of that ill-fed, skinny kid looking at the camera, with scared and haunted eyes, his jacket missing buttons and his clothes tattered, and then read those poems conceived in that childhood of beatings and tattered clothes, and written in youth.

He went to the Saint John *Telegraph-Journal* in 1963 on the strength of his editorial ability, to Fredericton in 1968 on the strength of his poetic genius, as writer-in-residence at the University of New Brunswick, after he won the Governor General's Award for a collection called *Bread, Wine and Salt.*

In Fredericton came his golden age, or golden moment—the flourishing of his genius, of his temperament, the legend surrounding both his enormous talent and his drinking. His poetry continued to change, to become more analytical, observant and objective; a strong narrative voice emerged, psychologically penetrating, always sympathetic to its subject. He was trying in a way for pure poetry—which meant pure truth. As always, humanity is everywhere in his work—in his world you cannot exist without it.

At his house on Windsor Street in Fredericton—called, of course, Windsor Castle—Nowlan entertained, met other writers and poets, started his pet projects and societies (the world was so utterly self-absorbed as round, why shouldn't we claim it flat); it seemed to have still had purpose then. So many of his friends were descendants of Irish and Scottish clans who had fought the British at every turn—why not reclaim the throne, even if in exile in New Brunswick?

He was interviewed about these claims by rather literal people who did not catch on to the seriousness of it all, or the joke. And Nowlan was a master of the understated in both.

Like the seriousness accompanying the joke played on the world when he was given the task, as a young man, of measuring the Hartland Bridge, to reassert its claim as the longest covered bridge in existence. Nowlan measured it from one side of the Saint John River to the other and then, for good measure, he continued across the street, proceeding until he came to a stop at his desk in the *Observer* office. Walking backward all the way, he finished his measuring when he was able to sit down.

And though he helped reassert the right to the throne for the descendants of Bonnie Prince Charlie, he was, in the end, no British hater—that was a small man's part. Besides, he cared too much about British literature and tradition.

Meeting Prince Charles in the 1970s, he commented that he liked his beard.

"But my mom disapproves," the Prince said.

"Ah, Sir, what mom doesn't?" Alden Nowlan offered.

When meeting June Carter Cash, he said, "Miss Carter, I have long been of the opinion that you have the sexiest right knee in all of show business."

"Thank you very much for noticing," Carter Cash said, and lifted her dress to show him the knee.

His parties were filled with people from disparate walks of life, who had totally different opinions and political stripes, who might not speak to each other anywhere else. At Alden Nowlan's they found safety. The premier could be there, and so, too, members of the Opposition; a single mother on welfare sitting beside a young corporate lawyer; sound poets adrift in the world, and young men with their daddies' money; rural-bred soldiers from Gagetown sitting beside urban pacifists wearing peace beads, sharing cigarettes from the same pack. As Gorky said of Tolstoy, so someone might have said of Nowlan: "As long as this man lives no one will be an orphan."

Of course he could not live. That is always the secret.

Someone once told me that Alden Nowlan only attracted young-sters, and that people his age were wary of him. Although he had a great many older friends, that is still true in part, but it was not Nowlan's fault. The young sought him out, as the young must have sought out Emerson or Socrates. Why? It is simple. The young have to.

He was comfortable with the young. They came to him because for many he was the first adult they had ever heard speak like an adult should speak. Many were would-be poets, and he was a mentor.

Some his own age, especially from the university, were wary of him because, just like Beethoven with the nobility, he could not bow easily to those who had not come to knowledge within the harsh life-and-death parameters he himself had faced.

But the young came. He never so much instructed them but lis-tened to them. Perhaps, who knows, they were taken seriously for the very first time in their lives. It is literally true that there was a time his house was filled with people young enough to be his sons or daughters.

I went down to meet Alden Nowlan, but the lights were out, and I did not want to wake him at the door. I turned my motorcycle around in the summer air, and shifted through the avenues of peo-ple already asleep.

He did not know of this impromptu visit, and the next time I visited was one of my very last.

He was watching Peter Ustinov's documentary on Russia: "'Lo, Davy," he said, and got up to turn the television off.

"No, Alden," I said, not wanting to disturb his program. "Please leave it on."

"Nonsense," he said. "If Peter Ustinov is on TV and David Adams Richards enters the room—off goes the television." And he made that great jerking motion with his arms.

I sat down. He was silent a long moment. Then he looked over at me and, with a kind of cherub-like smile, shyly added, "Mind you, Davy, if David Adams Richards was on television and Peter Ustinov walked in—well then, what I mean to say is, well, you know—the TV just might go off, too."

At the last of his life he was left alone, as old friends departed for other places and lives changed. The great court was over and often he sat in his den in solitude.

Some made excuses, saying he was difficult and his best days were over. Noble of them . . . to be entertained by him on his best days.

And he—well, he was still writing great poems, about the martyrdom of Bobby Sands, about going to a "school for the retarded" to speak to children, or summing up Boswell's two-hundred-thousand-word biography of his old friend Sam Johnson.

I have often wondered what Canada gave Alden Nowlan. I have never come up with a satisfactory answer.

In his great poem *Ypres: 1915*, he asked, in a curious way, if he even had a country—and more subtly, though never spoken, if Canada of today deserved the bravery of those kids fighting along the line, the first time the Germans used gas.

As I say, I do not know what Canada really gave him; but I know in my heart and soul what he gave it. He was the greatest poet of his generation, one of the few truly great literary figures this country has produced. But so like his literary hero Junkets, he always made an awkward bow.

I went down to visit Alden Nowlan, on that summer night long ago. Who knows, maybe to thank him. But it was too late, the curtains were drawn, and the lights were out.

He took a heart attack at his home on June 11, 1983, and, putting on old and tattered clothes that he would know from the days of his youth, walked unaided to the ambulance, just as he long ago told God he would do for Him—die with courage.

He slipped into a coma from which he never recovered, and died June 27, 1983, at the age of fifty. Two years younger than I am now.

2003

THE ALCOHOLIC VISION

IN *UNDER THE VOLCANO,* MALCOLM LOWRY'S PRODIGIOUS HERO, Geoffrey Firmin, drinking himself to death in Mexico on the Day of the Dead in 1938, has, as you may expect, memories of his past. They come to him in the form of spectres, "imaginary parties arriving," as he says; and his name is "repeated with scorn."

"Familiars" follow him about his garden as he searches under the sunflowers for hidden bottles, admonishing him for his wasted life. Memories also of those superior people who think they know the fault or the trick in what he says, when there is nothing but innocence.

Lowry's great creation—Geoffrey Firmin's ghosts and admonishing "familiars"—seem to be these kind of fellows. And so, too, were Firmin's ex-wife and half-brother on that fateful, atrophied day, so long ago in time, yet a moment in our imaginations.

Perhaps that's what intrigued me about Lowry's book. It is not so much that Firmin remembers ghosts as they present themselves to him, out of the blue, and bid him good-day. But before they bid him goodbye, they allow him to remember how casual is the damning of his spirit.

Lowry knew what it was like to be a convenient target: belittled as a child, terrified of sex, laughed at as an adult, deemed a failure by the literary world he loved, ousted from friends, betrayed by others, alone with self-contempt, he ran from ghosts most of his life, from city to city, bar to bar, friend to friend, leaving in his wake from England to New York to Mexico, to Dollarton, British Columbia, what he considered, as did everyone else, the sludge of inadequacy and failure.

Until finally in Canada in the 1940s he penned his masterpiece.

Before he ever got to write it, he was committed to an alcoholics ward in New York and lost his first great love somewhere along the way because he was too shy to kiss her.

Before he got to BC, Malcolm lived a life of drunken terror in Mexico. People on pleasure boats would see this lone figure swimming three miles from shore in the Gulf of Mexico's shark-infested water, his head bobbing up and down: "Trying, you see, to rid myself of old dad's spies," Malcolm would say happily when asked what in God's name he was doing swimming alone so far from land. His dad had him on an allowance from the estate, something like Poe's stepfather, and like Poe's stepfather, was suspicious his son was a useless weakling and wasting his life.

Here we have it, then: a weak-willed man on an allowance from pa, and about to write of the tragedy of all the world. Better in the end than Brendan Behan or Henry Miller, or Faulkner or Hemingway. More compassionate about both men and women than most of what passes for compassion today. As great, in my mind, as the two great figures of the late nineteenth and early twentieth centuries—Hardy and Joyce. Exclusively tragic and exclusively alone. Alone and self-conscious to the point of self-betrayal. Smirked at by authority both in police headquarters and publishing houses.

Would those who have literature catalogued into who can write what approve? An allowance from a rich, if self-righteous, father supposedly means a soft boy. A father who could afford to indulge him to an apprenticeship with Conrad Aiken? But Lowry came from a different age, an age that hadn't yet completed the tunnel vision about literary roles. Without being as determined as he was to overcome what he did, he might have settled into the role of literary gadfly, or English buffoon, or as one of those happy, exuberant men who is always welcome at a literary dinner party with the exceedingly wholesome writing wife of a tenured eccentric professor, because he knows the stories that have to be told to keep people entertained.

Of all the roles to play, buffoon is the easiest role in which to challenge the contempt of others, but the most difficult to escape from self-contempt.

In the end, however, Lowry's work, written isolated and alone, was as noble as the spirit of mankind. And he suffered dearly for it for thirty years.

He finally managed to write one of the four or five greatest books of the century. *Under the Volcano* is a book that is a map of our century's soul. As dark a book as you would ever want and hilariously funny (but those who want easy jokes or need to read a funny book to see humour won't get it and of course don't deserve to), and perhaps one of the very few great books about alcoholics. Certainly the greatest one. After you read Lowry, so much other writing about booze is as flat as dishwater and as conniving as a snitch.

Lowry, when he was down, was a panhandler, yes. A mooch when it came to booze and pills and anything else he could get into his mouth to take him away from where he was. A man who was terrified because he was isolated in his talent and vision, yet forever brave. He was incredibly strong—he knocked out a horse with one punch—yet insecurity made him a painful blubberer. A paranoid who had good reason to be. A man who found it hard to look at women without blushing. Yet a man who loved women dearly. The first time he met his second wife, Margerie, at a bus stop in Los Angeles, he put his arms about her and hugged her for over an hour. Margerie was there through thick and thin. Sometimes when he was working, he would look over a paragraph he had just written and say, "Margerie, could you please come here and tell me what in hell it is I mean by this?" Loners are such because they are forced to be, not by temperament alone, but on occasion by talent. The crowd doesn't want them or need them, and in one way or another bullies them out. Lowry's success in literature was as remarkable as Disraeli's in politics. Nothing was in his favour except genius.

Lowry had to convince himself to keep at it. Here, being suicidal is not a weakness so much as a bedrock foundation. As Seneca knew, thoughts of suicide make a comfort in dire times. Seneca had to deal with Nero, Lowry with literary obscurity. Both were damned in their own time.

On one occasion, Lowry lay in bed for three days without energy to eat or speak or drink after the book was rejected for the third time. And then with Margerie encouraging him, he went back to work on his manuscript once more. It's what kept him alive. He must have remembered his promise even though the world had given up on him. The promise of youth, when people recognized his genius before he had written a word.

When he was twenty-two, Lowry told eighteen-year-old Dylan Thomas that someday he, Malcolm Lowry, would write a great novel, one that would outlast Melville's *Moby Dick*. When he met Dylan Thomas years later in Vancouver, Dylan was getting all the attention as the world-famous drunken poet.

Lowry took to sulking and being moody and not answering questions and finally to breaking some of the light bulbs.

As much as I love Thomas, Old Malc—the "good-night disgrace," as Conrad Aiken sadly said to him—was the far greater writer. It's just that no one needed to care that he was. The twists and turns it took for him to produce his masterpiece are unknown.

He once complained to his New York agent that there were only two people in Canada who knew what in hell it was he was doing. As Douglas Day has said, that probably wasn't true. When the publisher in New York was hesitant to publish the book, after Lowry had worked on it for nine years, Lowry wrote perhaps the greatest defence a writer has ever given his own work. It was finally published in 1947 and acclaimed as one of the great works of the century. The *Globe* in Toronto called it "turgid."

It might be fitting that our "national newspaper" so disparaged a book in such a provincial way. And what could Lowry do, now that he was finally an overnight success? He could only try to find a bar, get drunk and hide.

What do you do when you write one of the great books of the century? The publisher waits for an encore, but it doesn't happen. By 1954 Malcolm was frantically writing his publisher from Italy, telling them he wanted all the copies they had sold of *Under the Volcano* back because he now knew more about alcoholism than ever before.

He still had moments where he wrote wonderful lines, a few really good poems, even nearly great poems; a story called "Forest Path to the Spring" is also very good. But he spent his last years running with Margerie by his side, back to wherever it was he could find shelter.

Once, he was put into an alcoholic rehabilitation program and given an aversion addiction treatment during which he was left in a room and allowed only alcohol. Most drunks lasted about three days. After fourteen days of drinking nothing but gin, Lowry was still going strong and felt, he said, "As fit as a fiddle." They finally had to haul him out. He confessed to Margerie he'd been so thirsty in treatment that he drank his own urine.

Finally he went to Ripe, England. And there he lived, drank little and endured the howling smiles of the well-gossiped, stodgy, pedestrian, flatulent high-school English teachers and rugby boys who had no idea who was in their presence. He would hide in the bushes and grin at them as they passed. But then, what would it ever matter, for finally a writer's work, if it's good enough, belongs to the stars.

And then in 1957 he died. Gin and pills and Margerie running out of the house because he had threatened her, coming back the next morning and finding him.

"Malc is gone," she said to the landlady.

"Where? Up to London?"

"No. He's dead."

He lies buried in Ripe, England. The coroner stated that his passing was "a case of death by misadventure."

1998

BRAVE AS ANY MAN

F. SCOTT FITZGERALD DIED AT THE AGE OF FORTY-FOUR. NO one, not even himself, meant to kill him. But there is no doubt in my mind that he joined the assault.

It was one way to get along and not have to try to be what he might have become. A failure is great if he can always pretend he could have succeeded to those who will sympathize. A drunk is almost always the personification of this. Sooner or later they all start lampooning themselves for laughs. After his early success he seemed driven to fail.

He began to applaud Hemingway instead of himself, became a script writer in Hollywood. People who worked with him thought he was long dead until they met him. Hemingway called him "a coward" to his former friends.

I admire Hemingway. I think all in all he was one of the great short story writers of the century. But most of us have at least one way to be a coward. When it really counted, and where it really counted, Fitzgerald was as brave as any man.

They told Scott to stop drinking, stop writing and he'd live longer. He did try with drink. He never, ever put down the pen. How could he? He was born to it. When you are born to something, you stop and you're dead anyway. Boxers know this, as well.

There is a great scene in the made-for-television film *Last of the Southern Belles* where Fitzgerald is in a speakeasy. Some men are making remarks about Ernest Hemingway. Fitzgerald stands up (he was no great hulk of a man) to defend him:

"My name is F. Scott Fitzgerald. I wrote *The Great Gatsby*. Ernest Hemingway is a friend of mine," he says. He gets his nose bashed in for his effort.

Hemingway would never have spent a second defending him. The secret is, Fitzgerald knew this.

Scriptwriting in Hollywood. But I suppose most people who know of Fitzgerald know of these stories. Because that's where the money was. He needed to impress Hemingway by writing letters about how much money he made; and then, feeling guilty about lying, he'd write a retraction.

As far as Hollywood went, almost nothing he did was put in the can. So he died a failure. Now almost everything he wrote is a movie of some kind.

Most writers, no matter where they are born, know this truism. You can TRY to be famous or you can TRY to be great—you choose, because you can rarely TRY to be both. Fitzgerald was convinced by others, or by himself, that he should not TRY to be great—deciding, instead, to become rich and famous. (Sometimes he dressed incognito even though no one knew who he was.)

He goes in and out of fashion, like all writers. There is only one person I admire who really thinks Fitzgerald was a great writer. But there is nothing Fitzgerald has done that I haven't respected. And I've respected him more over the years. I think the unfinished *The Last Tycoon* was an unfinished masterpiece.

And in a certain way, I've respected his life more than his writing, although his life was so wretched. His wife in an institution, and his daughter, "Scottie," in private school; dogged by debt and memories of what might have been, friends who had fled, hiding his bottles from his mom.

Never to be even a twentieth as good or as celebrated, I still could have humbly offered some advice. Being published at almost the exact same age, about a year before either of us shaved, we went along the same road for a while. Met many very well known people, most of them older by ten to twenty years.

I could have told him that he was once so young there was no way any of them was ever going to forgive him for any success he had. Nor, finally, did he have to take the blame for this. That the bottle is never in your corner, but is the best counterpuncher in the business. You hit it, it hits you right back, twice as hard.

He went off to Hollywood, hoping that newness, and money, was everything it was cracked up to be. But he was no longer new. He was sick and old at the age of thirty-six. In many ways forgotten.

There was a great confrontation between Dashiell Hammett, writer of *The Thin Man*, and Ernest Hemingway over Scott at a party one night. Hemingway was trying to show his prowess in front of Hammett, who, having worked as an agent for Pinkerton, was not impressed.

Hammett finally said, "Why don't you go back to bullying someone you're capable of bullying—Scott Fitzgerald. Poor Scott—the very best we have—if he only knew."

Hemingway left the room.

Some say Fitzgerald did know. If he did, other people's ideas of what he was always got in the way.

Hemingway used boxing as a metaphor for writing. In a way it's better than another metaphor used mainly by academic writers—baseball.

Writing is no team sport. I agree it is like boxing.

Both professions are lonely. Both are preyed upon by the vulgar.

Both have their entourages, ready to flee at a given moment. Both have their Don Kings.

Fitzgerald would have known all of this. There was something magnificent about his struggle to keep it all going.

Or to pretend to keep it all going while essentially throwing it away. *Last of the Southern Belles* is one of the great movies about a man who knew his reach should exceed his grasp and sometimes couldn't bring himself to reach.

Once in my life I was at a party with a person who knew F. Scott Fitzgerald. The year was 1985, and I was invited to her house in New Orleans. She was an old lady, a Guggenheim lady, who had known them all—Hemingway, Fitzgerald, Dorothy Parker, Faulkner.

At the party was a small—tiny, really—Southern gentleman by the name of Everette Maddox. He had written a collection of poems called *The Everette Maddox Song Book*. He looked like a ghost.

"I am a howling failure," he told me, and seemed pleased. His teeth were going and his body was frail. Really when you read his poems, you realized that he had two things to offer: first, a wide-eyed innocence about his own predicament—as if he alone couldn't believe how he'd ever gotten himself into such a wretched state; and second, a despair and a hope that he would someday soon disappear off the face of the earth.

He was drinking himself down to nothing as it was. He had started off at 150 pounds, with a wife, a job, a house and a car. When I met him, he was 109 pounds, no wife, no job, no house and he was unsteady when he walked.

He swept up at a tavern, and organized poetry readings.

Everyone he had ever loved had left him. And in a way he blamed no one. I will tell you I thought he was a great poet. One of the best poets I've ever met. But his life wasn't so great. It reminded me of Malcolm Lowry's short story about the ill-luck of writers: of Poe's disastrous relationship with his stepfather; and of Keats's early death.

The short story is called "Strange Comfort Afforded by the Profession."

Mr. Maddox was a Southern gentleman. There was an Old World romantic notion in him. There is a story that after he read a friend a new poem once, his friend was so moved he blurted, "I'll buy you a bottle of bourbon if you let me put my name on that."

Everette winced, looked around the room to make sure no one was watching and handed the poem over. His friend, who had just been joking, started to cry.

Everette kept waiting for everyone, especially his wife, to come back, tell him they loved him, all was forgiven. You can see it in every page of a poetry book that may have sold a hundred copies.

"Please come back," he wrote on my copy.

He died on a park bench in New Orleans at the age of forty-four.

Now they celebrate his life. Some say he was great. A wonder, a delight.

As with Fitzgerald, they were all happy he was dead so they could love him once more.

But really that's the nature of the beast. Even the writers themselves know this.

Once a young interviewer, on leaving my study, stopped to look at a picture of Roberto Duran training for his junior middleweight bout with Davey Moore.

"You know who that is?" I asked.

"Of course," she said, because she knew who my favourite writer was.

"That's Leo Tolstoy," she answered proudly.

I told this to Rick Trethewey, a friend of mine, a writer who was once a professional boxer.

"Tolstoy never got such a great compliment," Trethewey commented. He's right.

And Tolstoy knew what Duran knows.

There's always enough blood to go around.

1995

GRETZKY GAVE US EVERYTHING HE HAD

HE HAS HAD MANY NOMENCLATURES: THE GREAT ONE, GRETS, Number 99, the Wayner, and, on occasion, the Whiner. I was in my early twenties when I heard that a kid from Brantford was going to be greater than Bobby Orr. I didn't want to believe it. I'm not sure why. In a way, hearing how many goals he had scored in one year, (about a thousand and a half) was like hearing about the Krupp Cannon in the 1870s—which, since it fired accurately up to four times the distance of any other cannon of its time, couldn't be for real, and therefore was hard to sell to the Prussian army chiefs of staff.

In many ways Gretzky was a hard sell. I was part of those who waited to be convinced. For he was the antithesis of what a hockey player looked like. He was too small; supposedly didn't skate that well; supposedly again, had no shot; looked awkward; didn't really mix it up. So many of the greats looked better on skates, were bigger, could take the shot and had a mean streak. Bobby Orr (the only man who rivals Gretzky for number one) had a mean streak—and when he skated, my God.

———

Gretzky had to quell every doubting Thomas. For a while there were thousands, maybe a million. If his holding sixty-two National Hockey League records is a legacy, his more lasting personal achievement is that. I don't think there can be any more questions. He has answered them. Now, looking back at it, it didn't even seem that hard to do. He has proven that no player born on any soil was greater. Still, it must have taken its toll. He has aged before our eyes.

Much of the criticism wasn't even about hockey. There was something about his personality, too. He was too clean, shy, and his opinions seemed to be rehearsed. Yet he loved attention. Then he never got in trouble. There was always a bit of danger about Messier, which was appealing. For some, Gretzky was too close to his father. And after he went to L.A., he was seen to be mouthing the sentiments of the hockey commissioners to make the game more appealing to the Yanks. "Good for the game" is a line I've always mistrusted.

The game in Canada was on a decline and Gretzky had gone south, for the market—for the money. It was mentioned in the House of Commons as a national crisis. But a thousand other players had gone south over the years: Hull and Howe and Orr. Or was it just L.A. we felt didn't deserve that great a hockey player? But at one time they had Dionne. That is, our country has often given its national treasures away, bringing them home for the Order of Canada. Maybe we have no options anymore. But if we don't blame ourselves, we can't blame Gretzky. He stayed here longer than most. He also played some of his greatest games for Canada. I don't remember him ever saying no.

I don't know when I began to change my opinion about him. I still love the way Lafleur moved, and Mario played, Denis Savard, Doug Gilmour and Pavel Bure, too. But then again, there is only one 99.

One night watching a game back when he played for the Oilers, I suddenly sat up. He was there. And it was over—that is, my feeling that I ever needed convincing anymore. It had dissipated in his move behind the net, at centre ice, and when he came out from the corner and found—without even looking—anyone he wanted to, at any time, with a pass. I was as close to watching perfection as I was likely ever going to be. I was alone with no one to shout about it with.

He then, over twenty seasons, shattered all the records. I have delighted in his play for years, but saw him play live only five times. The first was the second game against the Soviets in the 1987 Canada Cup. The one that went into double overtime. Even greater was his moment in the third game, coming back from 3–0 and the pass to Lemieux with a minute left. Or the 1991 Canada Cup, when he seemed to handle the Swedes singlehandedly.

What to me was his greatest moment—the moment he made me proudest? I'll whisper it. It was when he sat alone on the bench after our loss to the Czechs in '98. I realized, at that moment, five o'clock on that dreadful morning, that in some truly ultimate way, he had given us everything he ever had.

So how will we measure the man? We will measure him by what we refuse to forget after he is gone.

1999

(I thought of this essay again, when in 2015 at the World Championship we dominated every team—especially the Russians; that we won both the World Cup and the 2014 Olympics. However, looking at the newspaper reports on the World Championship of 2015, and the texts and emails that responded to it, I realized how many Europeans simply believed that if the NHL hadn't been in the midst of the Stanley Cup at that time, the Americans would have won, their thinking being that all the players on US-based teams must be American, neglecting the fact that Crosby, Burns, Giroux and most of the Team Canada players played for US-based teams, as did over half of the Russian players, including Ovechkin. There seems no longer any way to correct a mistruth about us, which is simply taken as fact.)

2016

IN DEFENCE OF MY GRANDMOTHER

MY FATHER BY THE AGE OF FIVE WAS LEFT SOLITARY AND alone, raised by young girls his mother hired to take care of him when she ran the theatre business in our little town of Newcastle, New Brunswick. She loved my father, but as fate would have it, she was a widow and had a business to run. The maids used to terrify him, in conspiracy with certain people in town. One of the things they did was put him to bed and put the chair his father, who had died of diabetes in 1924, used to rock in outside his door, telling him that his father was now a ghost and watching him. Funny enough if you're a girl of seventeen full of piss and vinegar and rifling through rooms downstairs. Terrifying if you are a boy of four, believing that these girls are there to protect you.

It is amazing to me that women, and men (and for some reason more men than women), have written about independent women of the 1920s and 1930s, and have ascribed to them many of the fashionable sentiments of independent women of the eighties and nineties. That is, they have accepted the ideas and ideals of our time as being essential to an overall wisdom, and transposed these new virtues back to my grandmother's time and place believing this is the only way to portray women as being seriously independent. The crowds rock and roll with this, too, because they have the firm belief that "freedom" is something that can only be explained because our generation—our Western affluent generation—is the only generation wise enough to have achieved it. And that the fight for women's rights is somehow the one thing worth portraying, but only in the way acceptable to people who have learned the right lessons. Besides—and here is the catch—so many of these writers and thinkers have been told all their lives what to believe about the fight. And more to the point, what is now virtuous and what is not.

This prevalence is not considered false by many people I know and my concern about it is often viewed with facile enjoyment.

But there is a part of this that is so misrepresentative of the world I came out of some comment is necessary. Because I have noticed that some people are determined to use my grandmother's life in a way to prove their and my own generation's advancement or ascension. That they do and have done this with women of the thirties in novels written now by certain men from coast to coast does not bother me in the least—pandering to fashion is never out of fashion. But that they bring my grandmother into the fray is something else again.

Back in the mid-eighties, when I was attached to a university here, certain women lectured me about this: "Yes, your grandmother was just like me," they would tell me. Matched by a sympathy not one of them really felt. For they did not know her at all—and she would have seemed to them to be troublesome, because of how old-fashioned she was.

What's more my grandmother would have scared half of them to death, simply with her gaze. Yet back then in the mid-eighties what these entirely nice, competent young ladies were doing, or wanting to do, is to claim my grandmother's uniqueness as a parcel. That is, that her singular toughness and solitude were theirs for the asking because they themselves had enough money to be taught how to think. If that is unfair, tell me where it is unfair and I will work on correcting it. They were the daughters of lawyers or doctors and so often had been told how to behave—*not in order to be wise, but in order not to be left out*. Being left out was what they really couldn't accept. In fact in their certain circles so often others were scapegoated and left out. Religion was oppressive; men were the cause of it. Pregnancy was a crime (in many circles) and men were a cause of that, too. Sexuality could be, and should be, expressed by women but not by men—an affair was in order for a woman, but a man was a scoundrel if he succumbed. And the idea often rehashed was that one must look upon all of this with a good deal of irony—and if you challenged this assumption, as I did from the first time I heard it and from the first book I wrote, you were considered a chauvinist or a sexist—in fact you were not to have a voice in the great new debate.

Except the debate was not new, not particularly genuine and almost always self-infatuated.

What disturbs me, even now, is these young women, or many of them simply assumed my grandmother would have thought like they did—about the terrible Catholic Church or abortion; or more to the point, she would applaud how they now think as virtuous. Of course that is a completely false assumption, and a pernicious one. Or what is pernicious is many of them believed that what they could teach her she would soon ascribe to. That is, "I would have loved to

have talked to her," one young lady said to me, as if handing a bene-
diction. Well, perhaps she wouldn't have cared to talk to that young
lady. This naïveté followed them without much harm, but who
knows how they may have harmed others. It is also the lie deeply
embedded in conventional literature that those forerunners were
much like the runners now. What smugness laces up the shoes of
their sentiments?

"I would have liked to have met her," another woman said. "We
would have had so much in common—"

Well, not the Catholic faith, I gather; or not my grandmother's
hypocritical (they would say) devotion to it, I suspect; or not the
saying of the rosary during those often-lonely Lenten hours. Not
the moment when her adversaries tried to blow up her business. So
then I assume she was speaking of other, more lofty things. And of
course she was, and those lofty things were things she had learned.

Anyway, I suppose I could have told her my grandmother was
not much of a joiner, and she was from the time of twenty-four an
outcast—both things that weren't (and still are not) at all fashionable
with the civilly conscious university-bred young women and men I
came to know in those years.

As I remember it many of them scrambled (and still do) to be
included in a collective suffering where they were afforded all the
outrage of the higher moral ground. There was often among them
a huddling for safety, comfort and inclusion. In the literature the real
truth about people—women and men—was often (though of course
not always) clouded by picky and trendy leftist theory. Women cheeky
and all knowing never subscribed to male proclamations, but had
qualitatively different ones of their own. (That is why abortion is
such a revelatory thing in some of these books and films written by

nineties men about thirties women. My good God, any independent women of the thirties must have had one, or helped procure one, because their ethical base would have been in tune with women taking second-year social work in 1999. And if not, then they were not the real women—not the ones one would spend time with or write about.)

In fact most activists use theory as the means to transport themselves to a social advantage through a class disadvantage many of them have never suffered. The novels of many liberationists, women or men, attest to this. I remember that in the eighties and nineties many of these renegade young women (and men) not only took classes together but marched together—and then of course, when it became fashionable, exercised together, ran together. I am not so much of a curmudgeon. I am not saying anything against it. I am especially not saying that women should not have the same advantages as men. I am only saying that their rebellion was for all it's worth a class-mindful—very class-mindful—rebellion, which did not and does not include any other class but the intellectual. And from my experience the intellectual class is no smarter or more certain of the world than any other.

It would not and really never did include my own mother-in-law, who born in poverty few of them could have imagined cleaned houses and scrubbed floors—not for an instant. And of course not only her—most of the women I admired would be disenfranchised by those who kept saying they themselves were disenfranchised. Still, my grandmother came from the same world as my mother-in-law; would have known her very well indeed.

However, more than a few women I knew in my years at university would have used my mother-in-law's plight, and what is worse, insisted they had every right to use it—use her hitchhiking to and from work as an elderly woman—to promote their idea of inequality. But let me tell you, most of them I knew in 1987 would have been comfortable only with the women she served—whose floors she scrubbed and beds she made; and few of them would have stopped to give her a ride.

This intellectualization of a suffering not experienced allows us a certain carefully protected status.

For, unlike my grandmother, if it had cost the majority of these people too, too much, few of them would have had the courage to engage the world. Oh, some would and did. But here is a secret: most did not. Theirs was a collective ascendancy, and a protected radicalism. They were safe; and within the university structure they knew it. They knew they had entered hallways where the idea of blaming others for the ills of the world was grand theatre. They knew how to act bold and irreverent, caustic and in some ways shameful, and still be included at grad time. This in fact was their ascendancy.

In fact such an ascendancy was what was allowed from the mid-seventies on. And many women I knew back then gravitated easily to what was allowed. It was at times hallucinogenic how competent they were at mimicry and false outrage over any bump in their fairly privileged positions.

That is, many of them did not do what my grandmother did, and what so few women or men ever do: something independent enough to be not allowed. What I am saying is that within their set so many of them were terrified of what most people still are, and what independent—and they are few—women and men have always had to face, and that is *disapproval*. And many times *severe disapproval*.

It is also a condition vastly acceptable to pretend that the radical-ism you hold is not in fashion when if it were not in fashion, you would never have joined to hold it.

So many of them were so offended over such inoffensive things that they like the princesses they were could feel the pea of offence twenty-five mattresses down.

In these university hallways I came up against a censure of Catholicism that even in the bitter rural, untrained backbiting between Protestants and Catholics I had not experienced before. Because it was intolerance intellectualized, and in so many ways just as bigoted. It was in effect a mutually accepted social devaluing of a whole group of people because of their creed, which would be frowned upon if it was any other persons or creed.

"This is the one thing we can lay into with gusto" their eyes seemed to say.

What was and at times still is so disturbing about so many young women and men in that time at university was that they believed that the dislike or even condemnation of ordinary things like kind-ness, family, children—or especially kindness toward men—was a disintegration of their core values. To me that is falseness anthropo-morphized, yet poets and writers were invited into study halls to read and demonstrate this as boldly authentic.

But what some Canadian books hide or attempt to hide is how it is fashionable today to poach independent thought then revise and straitjacket it to fit their schoolboy parameters. So in their books, women like my grandmother would toss the statue of the Virgin aside, and come to a more acceptable view of the world—that is, the view the writer wants her to have. They would be predictably ironic and bold (my word, they talk about sex), outrageous and irreverent. And *predictable*, as Laurence's Hagar Shipley is predictable, is the word. In this way many writers still do what schoolboys have often done: silently dismiss my grandmother's true humanity for a mirrored one, but look virtuous and emancipated whenever they address an audience about her emancipation.

"You see, that's what women were really like back then."

No, my son, they weren't. They were far less a mimic and far greater a person. My grandmother never had the option to follow or the time to learn the prescribed rituals of independence. She never went out of her way to shock or be irreverent. She was too tough, and she had too much to do.

So if I take this as my argument, that the women (and men) who so easily attached the label "feminist" to themselves did what was allowed, I can elaborate just a bit, and say if it was allowed in the eighties, something else other than feminism was allowed in the twenties—and nine-tenths of them would have been compelled to only do what was allowed then, as well. They would have ridiculed my grandmother for working and laughed at Zelda Fitzgerald (if they had heard of her). There would be exceptions, of course, but the exceptions would be few—just as in any real world. Therefore most of them would have looked upon my grandmother as a fallen woman, and gossiped about her as such. Like those angry little girls she hired in good faith who let their boyfriends in the side door and set up mean little robberies of my father's few pennies.

I suppose I got argumentative when many of the feminists I met back in the eighties kept telling me that my grandmother was a forerunner of themselves. They said this pleasantly, as if they had proven something that I should celebrate. And were disappointed when I did not.

"In what way was my grandmother like you?"

"She was independent."

"Like you?"

"Well, yes—like me."

One particular woman I know had started in grade one, and went through high school, went to university until she became a civil servant, and spent her life at it. At all these points in her life she believed what she was told. She was a feminist in the age of feminism—how hopelessly brave is that.

My grandmother did not have those more affluent gifts. She was out of school in grade six, was a self-taught musician, married outside her faith, which was deemed scandalous, but remained a Catholic; was left a widow with three small children; ran a movie theatre, when it was considered disreputable for a woman to work (especially in a theatre); and at the age when that progressive young woman was told in her course on feminist theory she had been victimized, Janie, my grandmother, was dressing as a man at night and, armed with a large RCMP flashlight, left her children in the care of my five-year-old father and went out to protect her advertisement posters from being ripped up by boys her opposition hired. And she knocked more than one man cold, not because she disliked men—in fact she liked men a good deal—but she had to, to protect her signs. So the difference between these two lives is not a difference in degree—but there is a difference in kind, which is completely and forever dismissed by unwise people. This mistake allows a transference of moral justification from the workaday world of my grandmother toward the more accepted middle-class posture considered now to be the only fuel that ever sparked independent women.

I often felt some young women I knew in the eighties and nineties were filching from my grandmother, her dignity and independence, just like a drunk filches in a tavern by pretending to share the virtue and concern of other drinkers.

But examine this from another angle. Let us see my grandmother taking that same course in feminist theory—and staying as tough and independent as my grandmother was. No. It could not be done. That's the secret—for in order to be tough there has to be a self-determining and self-autonomous side that allows for unique thought —and few things regulated in a classroom ever chart that course. That is what is so distressing about what is now considered independence, what is so untrue about it. That is why many of those young women reminded me of characters from Turgenev's *Virgin Soil* and became the officious cookie cutter replicas of one another, determined never to smile as you passed by. For you were the enemy, the terrible masculine writer, even though all your life you loved women as much as they.

My grandmother's tragedy has often been reduced to movie sound bites that my father ran in our theatre without knowing how close these came to poaching my grandmother's life. From Norma Rae, to the sisterhood movies of Jane Fonda, to the self-glorifying Thelma and Louise (women can be violent; men are not allowed to be), they are in their easy summations of what virtue is, dogmatic and less free than one could imagine. Far less free than certain nuns I have met and liked.

And what is virtue finally for many of these liberation movies— it seems, at times, and many times, virtue is the disinclination to disagree with their new convention; the hesitation to take on false-hood if it comes from them; and the uncertainty of truth to remain truth, if truth disagrees with their censure, their disapproval and their own kind of misinformation. So in the end virtue becomes falsehood and untruth.

I have been told all my life that this is the way it was when men ran the world—a world of falsehood, contrivance and untruth.

I saw first-hand in my lifetime, most of the same things applied whenever women did.

2005

REFLECTIONS FROM THE POOLS

A LETTER TO ANTON: I HAVE TAKEN A TRIP WITH YOUR MOM down the Bartibog River after trout. It is in the late spring and the water is high. I could write about this, I suppose, and tell you how we found a small run below a pool called Toomey's Quarry, where as my green butt butterfly went across the water and disappeared, a trout came up and grabbed it and a bear appeared just above us, watching. I had to play that fish with an audience I was hoping did not disapprove. That was long ago, thirty-eight years ago now, and that is one of the few things I remember about that particular trip, except the wind came up and it was colder as the day went on, and the rocks burdened us so much Peg said she would never run Bartibog again. She had packed a little lunch, and had brought napkins and white wine and wore a nice hat. Was it that trip or another where I cut my leg? No, Anton, that was another trip, the day I had walked down the long hill to Aggens Pool on the lower part of Bartibog River and fell on a glass bottle that lay off to the side of the pathway I walked. Aggens Pool, which the boys all called (and the girls, too) Maggie Aggens Hole. I tore the sleeve from my shirt and wrapped my leg up, and continued on.

There is a song about Maggie Aggens Hole that comes from the age of your mom's uncles. It is sung to the Johnny Horton tune "The Battle of New Orleans." These were boys who lived and died along the Bartibog River and grew up to be as grand as any men you might meet. One who came back shell-shocked from Italy (that horrendous forgotten part of the Second World War) and saved money so he could pay for his own funeral because Veteran Affairs would not; that is, they cut his pension, and he was left alone and broke. Oh yes, it seems to me that's a part of fishing rivers, as well, for he haunted the rivers of my youth that I, too, remember as part of my past, a past drifting away like a solitary fisherman poling a Nor-West canoe down the Miramichi River at twilight.

Some nights you would see him walking home after dark, a string of trout from those hidden leafed-over pools deep in the Bartibog wood. In Bartibog I met the first real true fishermen. And went to Aggens Pool many times alone. It is one of the most beautiful trout pools in the whole Miramichi Valley, and here's a secret: it doesn't always produce, but when it does there are magnificent moments, clandestine, for in some way all great fishing is a secretive act—an act between you and God. Don't laugh at your old man, Anton, for when the fish takes, you will know I tell the truth. There are brook-run sea trout weighing upward of five or six pounds, and salmon migrate there in the fall; move upriver under the leaves turning golden in the frost, and lie silent in the cold water of Kennan or Green Brook Pool, or any of the other pools that have formed our Bartibog River. Eagles will soar in the blue sky, the feathers at the tips of their wings moving just slightly in the currents of air far, far above us. If it is early enough in the day, the sun will light off the ice-covered boulders and seem like fire through the alders, the wind will only blow a little and you might see a buck in rut against the morning slopes, or a bear meandering away into its den for winter. Anton, I know you might think that autumn is a strange time to fish, but when the sun does its job and warms those boulders, the fish begin to move and a bright patterned fly will work. I have seen men take a fishing rod, some butt bugs and flies and, packing a shotgun in their canoe, pole down the river from the Bailey bridge that crosses the river near the highway, to Green Brook Pool, and onward to Kennan and Toomey's Quarry, watching for partridge on the wooded slopes, for salmon moving up the winding rocky river just at dusk.

I fell out of the canoe that day with Peg, that day in springtime so long ago I look upon us as children now. You see, it was growing late and I had managed to take a few trout, and Peg had picked a bag of fiddleheads on the warm riverbanks at midday, moving from patch to patch through the spring grass, like women have done for hundreds of years. Later we moved downriver with the sun in our eyes. I began to look around her to see how the water was bundling to rapids below us. Night was coming on, and we had another four miles to our old car.

"Where is it?" I finally said.

"Where is what?" Peg asked.

"You know, that rock."

"What rock—everywhere I look I see rocks—there is not a place on the whole Bartibog River I don't see rocks."

So I stood in the stern, to see where the hidden boulder was, that boulder just below the gravel-pit pool—everyone who has ever been in a canoe will know the one I mean. But when I stood, I saw, alas, we were right upon it. Son, I went flying into the air over your mom's head and into the water, with a kind of embarrassing *ker-splash*. Shadows played across the water in the late day, and I had to take off my clothes and dry them out on the rocks of the riverbank.

There is a poem by the great Newfoundland romantic bard Al Pittman called "Once When I was Drowning."

I almost drowned trying to cross the Northwest Miramichi River later that same June. I went down in my chest waders just above Little River Pool, a magnificent pool on the main Northwest Miramichi where I took a twelve-pound salmon in late June that year. The water was still high at that crossing and I felt my legs go out from under me when I became tangled up in rapids. I tried desperately to keep my balance, but you know me on my feet—I had no luck. Down I went in my chest waders. The pressure from water rushing into my waders caused my body to turn in complete circles under the water, my feet bobbing. But I shoved my arms against the river bottom and managed to right myself, and then swim across to the shore, my waders weighing an extra seventy pounds and my rod in my left hand. (I was alone at the time and this was an incident I was not going to tell anyone, but it is something that has happened to so many of us that not telling you seems silly; besides, I am not bothered by my own silliness anymore.) I took off my waders, walked down to the little river pool and on my fourth cast hooked a grilse. But the fish jumped three times and spit the hook.

I was lost in the woods half a dozen times, once trying to find a better way into Cedar Pool on the Northwest Miramichi back in 1982.

Cedar Pool was such a grand pool back then that a dedicated fisherman would do almost anything to get to it (the winter years have changed it and now it is not as good). There are rapids flooding over boulders at the top, very heavy water in spring, and it's hard to cross to where one must fish from the other side, but salmon lay from the rip that is about midpoint of the pool down to where the large, flat rock sits just near the bottom end.

Your godfather Peter McGrath and I decided to cut straight through the woods from his camp, and got so completely turned around, so totally bamboozled, that we finally had to do something unusual—we had to look at our compass, and came to realize we were going in the one direction we did not believe we were going in, a direction away from both the great Northwest River and an old nineteenth-century logging road we had walked along just a half an hour before. Once we realized our mistake, we were back on the logging road we had left, within ten minutes.

We tented on the rivers of my youth—that is, the south branch of the Sevogle and the Northwest Miramichi many times—in June or July back in those days, fishing for salmon. You mom's cousin David Savage and I ran Green Brook, that fertile brook cut out in the Bartibog wilderness that runs down to Green Brook Pool on the Bartibog, a half mile above the Bathurst Highway; ran the Northwest and the Little Southwest Miramichi, took fish (trout and salmon) on all those rivers. Twenty to thirty years ago now. And along Renous River and along the Main Southwest Miramichi, as well. I fished the conjunction of three great rivers, called Square Forks, perhaps one of the most pristine fishing areas in the world. I am proud of that. And I am proud, too, of releasing more fish there than I ever kept.

On the Northwest Miramichi, Peter and I ran a canoe at least once a year from the Elbow Stretch on the Northwest to the village of Wayerton, a distance of about fifteen miles, the great water teeming with young salmon—grilse—moving up, following the big salmon in. We would camp halfway down, make up a fire on the beach, drink our tea, listen to the water in the darkness, and now and then look up at the stars. We would beat that water to death for fish. Years before us, a friend of your grandfather told me he would run the same stretch of river at the same time of year. He and his brother would pole down in a ragged old canoe, hook into a dozen salmon and huge sea-run trout and never meet another soul. That was an age before Peter and David and me, and as you know, our day is now an age ago.

I will also let you in on a secret. There are very few people I would trust with my life. David Savage and Peter McGrath are two.

The Northwest Miramichi was the river where I learned to read a pool and know the hot spots in it. I took my first salmon from that branch, strangely enough with the first cast I ever made. That was far above Cedar Pool and far above the Elbow Stretch, as well; miles of wilderness, of rushing water and jagged hills. We travelled on woods roads so overgrown that branches would snap the truck mirrors off or at times punch a light out.

That seemed all a part of it back then. So, much of the hilarity of our youth was not spent in vain.

It was June 22 over forty years ago. We were at Brandy Landing Pool—B&L Pool, as it is known to Miramichiers.

I cast my first cast. Not a very good cast, either, but felt my line tighten instantly. I was using a red butt butterfly, number 6, with stiff wings. I had in my hands my first nine-and-a-half-foot Fenwick rod.

The rapids at the top of B&L Pool broaden out into dark, deep water where fish rest after their journey up the Stony Brook Stretch of the Northwest Miramichi, but my first cast was right into those turbulent rapids at the very top of the pool, so that particular fish must have been moving through. It was a male grilse; that is, a small salmon, about four pounds. I did not foul-hook him; he took hard.

The next spring—June 4—I took two large salmon and five large trout one evening at that same pool, standing only a few yards down from where I made my first cast the year before. The sea-run trout had come in amid the big salmon, and Peter and I were lucky enough to find them. Peter caught five trout that evening, as well.

B&L Pool is at the top part of the Stony Brook Stretch, in the deepest and most rugged part of the Northwest Miramichi Valley. It is a long bank to climb up or down, a hard pool to get to, and as I write this, it is many miles away. But we went there in late spring and early summer for almost twenty years, listening to the water roar beneath us, as we walked over the long, sweetly shaded hill, meeting very few other fishermen. Anton, I will tell you—I guess I have been as content there as any place I have ever been.

The woods have drawn me since I was a boy, and in many ways when I am there, I am a boy still. I can sit for hours in the shade of elms and birch. I watch others fish. And am just as content as if I were fishing. At one time lots of things mattered to me that do not matter much anymore. Son, I have had enough fame to know it is a lie. And, except for being with my family, I am most content when I am by myself. The woods and waterways of the Miramichi have kept me alive.

I told my brother this past June that I now understood why our uncle Richard went into the woods as a boy of twelve, and remained a woodsman all of his life, appearing at the doorway of my grandmother's house at ten at night, coming out from some solitary camp way up on the river and then being gone before breakfast the next morning, to come out again three weeks later.

He had much work to do.

That is, your great-uncle Richard Adams was a salmon guide on the Matapedia. And many say he became the greatest salmon guide of his generation, guiding presidents and movie stars. He carried Farrah Fawcett on his back across a river, guided Jimmy and Rosalind Carter. And sometimes I get letters from people as far away as Pennsylvania asking me to tell them of my many memories of fishing with him. I would gladly do so, but I never did fish with him. The memory I have is that one day he carried me down to the Matapedia River and put me into his twenty-six-foot Restigouche canoe to have my picture taken when I was four years old. He never drove a car; he never had his own house. He would hitchhike wherever he went. He told people who bothered to ask that he had heard that I was a writer of some merit, though he did not know much about me. But one day not long before he died, someone I know visited his place to do an interview. The fellow spied three piles of news clippings. When Richard left the room, the fellow took a glance at them. One pile contained stories on the Atlantic salmon. The second were stories written about Richard Adams. The third pile was stories he had collected over the years about me.

Three years ago a man from Boston sent me Richard's picture, his face chiselled out as if from granite, the shock of white hair to his shoulders, the old hat that had become emblematic of his life.

I have deep respect for the best guides.

An old guide visited Peter and me once years ago, after we ran an upper stretch of the Northwest Miramichi River called the North Pole branch, searching for trout. He came in to sit in our camp at night, and we bragged to him about having come down that hard run all the way from Lizard Brook, having poled the canoe across flats and through rapids. He spit his snuff into the fire and nodded. Then he commented shyly and politely:

"But youse see—the best thing for youse to do is pole yer canoe 'up' river nine or ten mile beyond that brook. That's where the trouts really is. When I was a boy, I would pole up there against the rapids and find the fish. I would camp out fer days up there. I had an old rod and some three or four flies. Some trout up there went seven pound."

You can imagine we did not think our own journey so exceptional after that.

The very next year—I think I was twenty-seven or twenty-eight—I walked three miles of river in my bare feet because I had torn my sneakers apart on the rocks. So both my feet were cut—but not as bad as one might think. Late that evening, just before I got to my truck, Peter managed to take one fish far below a pool called Moose Brook on the Depo Stretch of the Northwest Miramichi River, a stretch of water above the Stony Brook Stretch. That was the year I began to fish brown bug, with orange hackle, and it became my favourite fly, for I knew fish would show for it even if they did not take. Besides, I was never a great caster and a bug seemed to compensate for that fact.

And then I could tell you this.

For almost fifteen years I had a dog named Roo. Well, Roo travelled in my truck, shared my adventures and my baloney sandwiches, drank pop out of my cap, licked my face whenever I caught a fish, sat on the rocky banks as I fished a pool (laid up on the supplies in the middle of the canoe when we ran the river). At times in those years she was as close to me as any person, my only companion along the distant rivers, and except for my wife and kids, I loved her most. Where I needed her most was on the south branch of the

Sevogle River when I fished it alone. Down over those great spruce hills one is in solitude and there are many days you might not see another soul.

It is place of retreat, wilderness, where the fishing is best in late July and the black flies are ferocious. Three Minute Pool, Disappointment Pool, Island Pool, White Birch, Teacup Pool, Milk Jug. I have been fortunate to take fish from them all. And by fish, I mean salmon.

The best thing about the south branch is that you don't need waders; the water is warm enough to fish in sneakers and jeans (though still cool enough so the fish are active). It makes travelling over the slippery boulders easier. And so you can wander along its harsh and slippery banks unencumbered. If I travelled a long way from where we parked and it was late in the day, I would simply say "Truck" and Roo would turn and go, leading me back up the narrow pathways to the overgrown road, stopping to patiently wait until I caught up. I know I would not have made it back without her. Even when she had arthritis, she would hobble with me down to those tea-coloured pools of mornings long ago. Yes, she is gone now, but somehow still with me when I think of her.

This past June I spent a night showing your brother, John, how to tie a blood knot. I used to tie them quite a bit when I used a tapered leader. It is a valuable knot for him to know, just in case he wants to lengthen his leader and I'm not around. We are going into the Stony Brook Stretch with my older brother for two days. The water will be high now, and I know it will be hard fishing. It has been raining intermittently for a week or so, and I have watched it from our old farmhouse near the mouth of the Bartibog. Each day the clouds seem lower in the northwest sky, and the trees toss in the wind.

I am hoping John will catch his first salmon somewhere along the Stony Brook run. I am hoping that this is the year. He grew up in Toronto and has been to the water only three or four times. Two years ago we ran the Northwest on a day in early July and I hooked four fish, but he had no luck. I handed him the rod so he could feel in his arms how beautiful and powerful and majestic a salmon is.

So Anton, your brother arrived from our house in Fredericton the day before. I took him to the Bartibog, and we went to Aggens Pool. The water was high there, and no fish would take. In fact he could hardly walk in his waders far enough out to cast a line. I remembered the trip where I had cut my leg. I was then almost exactly the same age as he was that day, and it was only a week from the same day of the year.

"How many trout did you catch?" John asked, after we fished for three hours without seeing even a small fish roll.

"I caught seven that morning," I said, "all nice trout. But you will have your day—you will have many days," I said.

Well, I hoped and prayed that might be true. But the road to Aggens Pool is now a harder road down and we need a four-wheel drive to get in. A beaver pond has flooded the very path where I fell and cut my leg open, and a four-wheeler track—something unheard of when I was John's age—cuts through to the pool from the right side. Poaching is rampant on the river now, Anton; trolling for fish at the mouth; nets strung across pools far upriver, where wardens almost never venture. And bass are in the river, in ever larger schools.

That night it was still raining hard, down against the raspberry bushes, and the clouds were dark. There was a smell of lilac in the wind and the grass was green all down the four acres that we own here.

The two water barrels at the side of the house were full, and now and again lightning would flash almost splendidly against the far-off pines, and thunder rumble far across the great Miramichi Bay.

So I painfully showed him the knot. Still, John catches on to things. He is a good mechanic and a great carpenter. In an hour he was tying blood knots as good or better than I was.

"Like this?" he asks.

The next morning the storm had rolled away, and we went in my brother's Jeep, and the road into Stony was different—you know, I simply forgot how long a way it was, and there was a new camp from the last time I was there, oh, such a long, long time ago now. But taking one look at the water I felt it was too high yet. I knew there would be fish here, but I thought: They will be moving through—resting farther up toward B&L Pool.

That did not mean we couldn't hook one. But after the first day we had not. We fished the home pool, and crossed the river in high water and went down to the pool below. The wind always comes up the valley after one o'clock and makes it very hard to cast—especially for John, who is just learning (but he is doing better and better each day).

John has heard so much about Stony Brook Stretch over the years, during those winter days in Toronto, with its sound of buses and subways, I was hoping for even one fish to show. But the great Miramichi River can break your heart, and yes, it often does.

We crossed the river again, and late in the day, after supper, went to the pool above the camp. It is a beautiful pool that bends left over big rock and you cast into the long, deep run that results. But it was roaring water. Hard to work your fly when your line is carried so swift and straightens too soon. The wind had died, as it always does in the evening, and two deer came out to munch at clover upriver by a hundred yards.

Finally we decided to call it a day.

I was using a wading stick given to me by Dr. Cole, an old fishing pal from days gone by, when I fished the great Square Forks, and I certainly needed it to cross back in the heavy current just at dark. John and my brother Bill managed to cross on their own. Anton, you know they have better balance than I.

Still nothing to show for all that but a small trout.

I told John there would be fish tomorrow.

We woke early.

I did not fish that day. It does not matter to me now. You see, sometimes if you are very lucky, you realize that very little matters except those you love. In fact, nothing else. I am less inclined to rush toward the water, knowing it will always be there when I get to it. And the wind was hard, blowing the water into a kind of endless chop; the sky was dull and grey and then brightened. I went up along the road, collected some firewood, brewed tea for lunch and boiled a piece of grilse we had from last year.

I walked through the woods to each pool, looking down into them with my Polaroid sunglasses, trying to see fish moving, but I could not tell in the wind. I know friends of mine like David and Peter probably could. I sat out in the sun and ate my lunch, drank black tea. So I watched a chipmunk chatter, its tail in the air, and said hello to a birch partridge, which swore at me up and down while trying to protect her three chicks. About four in the afternoon my brother saw fish moving up beyond the home pool. But they weren't stopping.

He and my son worked every pool again—all day. The water had dropped. But not enough.

Another two days, I thought as we sat out at the fire that night—then it will be great fishing. But we had only one morning left.

That night the stars came out and I remembered running the river with Peter thirty years before, stopping halfway down to pitch a tent.

So I thought about what to do, and I said the only pool to go to was B&L. The last pool up on the Stony Brook Stretch, a hard pool to get to still. Especially hard from this side of the river.

Bill hesitated and finally said he did not want me to go.

"I would prefer you not go," he said. I knew that was coming, Anton. Maybe you knew it, too. I guess I had been waiting for it all year in one way or another. From this side of the river, we would have to go over the bank on the far side of the pool, a horrendous climb, and then cross the river above the falls. It was the long vertical climb back up that worried Bill. The problem—well, it was not a problem to me, but to your uncle Bill—was the two heart attacks I had in the last year. It is not something I worry much about—and I do not want you to ever worry about it for my sake. Still, Bill did. I knew he would say this, so I drank my tea in silence and looked up at the stars, coming out now in the brilliant night. How many, many, nights have I loved this water?

"It's my heart," I said. "And it feels pretty sound—and if I do die, I will die at B&L—what better place on the whole Miramichi could I find?"

"I'm not having it," Bill said. "David, we're forty miles from anywhere."

I told him it was a foolish worry, that I could make that climb. But he would not give in.

"If you don't want us to go, we won't," John said.

I shrugged, spit the last of my tea into the fire.

"Don't be so damn foolish," I said. "What does it matter besides you having a chance at a fish. Bill and I both want that—but watch how you cross that river; don't go down in your waders there!"

The next morning I woke John and handed him one of my boxes of flies.

"Look through them," I said. "Take that green machine that Dave Savage tied me. It will work up there—you will see fish."

That day, of all days, they forgot the camera on the camp porch, and I ran up the road to give it to them, but they had gone. I did not hear the truck again for almost four hours.

Anton, I want to tell you something. Crossing the river at B&L is not too tough most of the time, but in high water it can be. When you cross a river, it is always the boulders one does not see that will tangle you. Sometimes they are right in front of you, but the swirl below you is at times as black as tar, capped by white spray rushing by. So I wondered if the crossing would be easy or tough. This is what I thought of when I sat there. I knew every inch of that pool, too, and wondered how they would fish it. Where John would step into it, and how he would work his way down.

Then I went for a walk back upriver. I ate my lunch staring at the water, and smelled smoke from a forest fire I hoped (and actually prayed) was not close.

But all things work out. I give you my word. Now, I did not see my oldest boy catch his first fish. But he caught it using a green machine our friend Dave Savage had tied. John crossed the river of my youth at the same age I had, and fished the same pool. But it wasn't the pool where he got the fish. It was the run 250 yards below the pool—a run my friend and your godfather—and one of the finest of woodsmen, Peter McGrath—had discovered back in those early days years ago. The run we would fish once a day for three weeks every year. My brother had told John to go and try it. So John walked down to it. He put on new leader and tied a blood knot. He stepped into the water, and waded halfway across the river before he cast. And he was beginning to cast well. On the fourth cast, Anton, his line tightened, and a young salmon, the same size as the fish I caught forty years ago, almost to the day, jumped high in the splendid morning air.

"Bill," he called, "I'm not sure, but I think I have a fish on."

And so he had.

Anyway, we drove home later. It was mild. There was the smell from a fire in Quebec, a hazy smoke all across the river where I have spent so much of my life. Peg was at the door, smiling like that girl who ran the Bartibog with me thirty-eight years ago.

Your mom's gentle smile made me realize that all things are possible. My son, there is nothing ever to fear.

I will get to B&L again. Roo and I will clamour down the banks of the great river together. Me with a rod in my hand, she stopping to wait as we make our way.

I believe that's the way it will be.

Someday, soon.

2015

KNOWING CANADA:
A RURAL PERSPECTIVE

THE NATION HAS CHANGED SINCE THE TIME I WAS A CHILD. I DO not know if it is for the better, but there is no doubt it attempts to be for the better. We are no longer a rural world, and for some reason that is looked upon as good. But in some sense we must realize that not being rural always was looked upon as being good, even when most of us were rural. That sophistication could only be seen in urban centres. And even when Toronto would have blushed to have called itself "a world class city." Even then—or I might say, even more so then—those in the rural world were always preached at in a certain way. Told in subtle ways that they had to smarten up, to become party to the great ideas, and that the great ideas were only the urban-centric ones. And even though some rural people were smart enough to realize that so much of sophistication relies upon a lack of nobility in the soul, we were still told we should strive for it. What I noticed was that if we did not adopt these ideas, we were part of the problem and not the solution.

The ideas that filter through to those of us in the supposed hinterland have always been slightly high-handed, the values slightly different, the wordlings who write in papers remarkably colloquial by pretending to understand and to know the hallmarks of success and to define Canada's role in it. That is, the first thing so many urbanites trade in for sophistication is common sense.

A thousand times I waited for the CBC to evoke the mystery in the Canadian man and woman that makes us great. Most of the time when I was growing up, they fed us with uninspired tributes to urban life, urban writers, feeding us sympathy for catchy and trendy ideas that came from south of the border.

But so much of Canada gives itself away—teeters on the brink of euphoria if mentioned by Hollywood, or in a New York paper, while at the same time pretending to scoff. Canada hates to be viewed poorly by its southern cousins. Therefore Canada tries—or at least tried when I was a boy to hide its real self from Hollywood, New York. There was little we could celebrate in rural Canada, unless it was the First Nations. We can't be seen to be rural, uncouth people—we have to know—yes, and know in the exact way others supposedly know. This was a problem for me when I was coming to age and waiting for some sign that defined not who I was but defined how those speaking to us knew who we were.

But they so often defined us by ignoring whole sections of the country they did not know, and worried us rurals would show them up. I remember a professor of economics from Calgary asking me blithely in 1990 whether or not I could fly from Toronto to New Brunswick—astonished that New Brunswick (home of the man who, as minister of aircraft production in the Second World War, oversaw the manufacture of six thousand Spitfires in four months) had an airport. I remember a young man from Vancouver, with the required love beads and long hair and almost all the in-vogue sayings, being dumbfounded to discover that I, who had met him in Spain and travelled with him, was actually a hick from New Brunswick, who could outclass him in history and literature and world affairs when I was nineteen years old.

"Really—New Brunswick—my God!"

It is no longer that way today, people assure me. Though I am not entirely sure. Nor should I be.

When I was younger, this inexperienced presumption afforded a most amazingly silly trait: that of watching how my sophisticate brothers from more cultured provinces longed to be defined by things.

Like a chimpanzee collecting hats and cigars to look the part.

That is, the things half of ordinary Canada wanted to define themselves by and show pride in were never ours to begin with. Game shows, television series, even fast-food restaurants.

The Price is Right, Let's Make a Deal—that's what I heard about when I was younger by people coming from Ontario to New Brunswick in the summer, who relaxed in cottages by our bay.

"We have Arby's where I come from—you should try my Arby's," someone from Ontario once told me with great glee when I was fifteen.

Of course Arby's, like McDonald's or anything else, was neither his nor Canadian. That he did not know this, or did and tried to keep it from both of us, seems a continual refrain by many Canadians who live in a world where they simply accept the premise that it is always good or better to be someone else.

I remember that when I was very little, I had great faith in our country. Or I should say, a different kind of faith—one that rested on the precept that if I did not know my country, it might, just might, know me. That is, I still believed I was welcomed in it. I do not think that as much now. That does not mean I do not love Canada—I do. It does, however, mean that Canada's major sentiments toward much of what I love have diminished over the years, so the country is now another country, its concerns, concerns I do not share and sometimes oppose. The sentiments Canada has aren't declared, set in stone—and millions of people like me do not share them. But you see, there is a feeling that in order to be proper Canadians, we should share them. Laughter at hicks and rednecks is always celebrated, and so we should laugh at those people we loved and grew up beside, who for the most part are as energetic, intelligent and as worthy of respect as anyone else I have come to know. But there are those we are not allowed to laugh at, satire or ridicule even at their most absurd. And most of us know who they are.

Back then it was different.

We were Maritimers, of course, and New Brunswickers to boot—but we were, at least for an identifiable moment in my childhood, back in those days of the fifties, Canadians first. There are very few times I now think of myself as Canadian first—Canada has tried by its culture and much of its literature to silence most of what I care about.

I love my country. So this is not meant to be seditious. However, I thought I was a Canadian for a little while. At five years of age, I had the big picture. We fought in a war, and way over in Korea—which I was informed was not quite a war, though many families had sons or husbands who'd bled and died in it. And we were all diehard fans of a hockey team: Montreal for me, and Toronto for my friends. But if this hockey team was Detroit, Gordon Howe knew where he came from; if Chicago, so, too, did Bobby Hull—and every other player who plied away in a foreign country for the glory of our national sport. (Americans still cannot seem to fathom the idea that someone from Canada could be a lifelong Detroit Red Wings fan, not knowing that every player playing for them up until the early eighties came from places like Thunder Bay.)

Though New Brunswick did not have an NHL team, nor ever would, our national sport was played out in arenas all across the province by men who, though not quite NHL calibre, had the hard edge of the great sport in their blood.

We were also back then a lumbering and fishing and mining community in a nation of such communities, and we belonged to a people still demonstrably rural.

Rural and in relative solitude—our provincial capital, which was just a speck on a map in the larger scheme of things, 120 miles away through woods and across the tributaries of at least two great rivers. The roadways had been built by lumbering companies well over a century before, and had become King's Highways over time. All evoking a kind of innocence and romance, I suppose no more innocent or romantic than anything else. Now there is nothing left of that. Our towns are ghosts of what they once were. Our rivers are closed in part to fishing. Forestry is depleted; the mining is gone. Car dealerships and fast-food chains dot our landscape. Our televisions beam in programs from other nations. And unless we leave, we are alone.

It has been said that two things kept our country together: CN Rail and CBC Radio. To say this means certain things to me. One is that we had no formal internal traditions that captured the imagination of the entire country, no real defining moment, and therefore searched for one, and found it in a symbol as prosaic as our national railway; which is good enough, when complemented by a radio service that went to the ends of our domain. But this concept allowed the idea of self-inflicted isolation—snow blowing over the diesel engines and a radio playing in some remote hamlet in the North. That is fine by me, if those on the radio really knew the people walking the tracks.

I suppose the idea that the CBC went to the ends of our domain, to igloos in the North and some lonely lighthouse on the east coast—when internalized was itself special, and evoked a kind of sweet hubris. But that hubris failed me over time, for over time I realized that three-quarters of the people who promoted this identity did not at all embrace what they said this identity held. That is, it did not hold or understand Canada, except with an asterisk. Many who rejoiced in these emblematic symbols hadn't been east of Montreal, and many used their limited knowledge of Canada in a way to promote themselves as truer Canadians. An Ontarian was a truer Canadian that those from my province, certainly. Quebeckers were, as well.

That has been the feeling since I was ten or more—and it is a legitimate one—that those in cities felt that they had the goods on how to be a citizen. And whether it was Quebec joie de vivre or Ontario Orange, it seemed exclusive and more than a tad smug. For the most part a connectedness in Upper Canada was based upon a shared economy and a moral disapproval of America.

We fit in on the periphery—we were mentioned by our urban brothers in passing. I suppose we had the rail and the radio to keep us together in all of this.

This threadbare connectedness showed our patriotic limitations, and both institutions, the rail and the radio, in a serious way were outmoded by the time I was ten. The radio hung on, and did so in a way in which its very dawdling, its very preciousness and prescribed sense of itself as a righteous opposite to TV—its issue-orientated talk shows with the same left-of-centre issues discussed—kept it alive and gave it a track record that is admirable—like NPR radio is admirable to millions. It is where the country that had no voice in film or movies got to listen to Canadian filmmakers vying eternally for a few dollars, where Canadians who always believed (as everyone) that a movie version somehow validated a book got to listen to writers who often pretended they didn't want their books made into films.

In my childhood passenger trains came in three times a day, and once when I was very little, I caught the midnight train to Montreal. On that train I drank a drink called 7up, and met an elderly black man who spoke French. I remember being assured of my provincial status when we came to a town not much bigger than my own. I revelled in the fact that we were now in Montreal—and grabbing my cardboard suitcase headed toward the door. This caused general amusement at the boy's expense. But the train back then held many country bumpkins just like myself.

The CBC was listened to when we were away from town and could not get our own station, called CKMR back then and managed by the father of a friend, and which had a range and a radius of so many tiny miles.

Listening to the CBC when we went fishing along Church River on Victoria Day weekend leaves me with a slightly abstract and conflicted feeling about the solitude, about the sense of isolation. It seemed isolation always had something to do with strained classical music and a report from the wheat board, and the rather austere moralizing and august voices about such things. The moralizing traits of these somewhat Social Credit voices, voices that often missed the point, confusing middle-class activism with moral justice, swelled the CBC ranks by the time I was twenty years of age, so I found it more and more difficult to listen. It might be a leap to say—but not a great one—that by the time I was writing my early novels, I realized many at the CBC felt that one couldn't believe in social progress unless they knew something about fine white wine and delicate cheese. The trouble is many even now wouldn't notice this as an affectation.

Back when I was a child there'd be patches of snow still in the woods, kids lining in a row to toss small lines hoping for big fish under the black rushing water of spring, with the scent of lilacs and the promise of sunshine up behind those still-turbulent, northern storm-tossed clouds. We might hear from the car on the bank where my friend's father sat watching us the sounds of mid-afternoon Mendelssohn coming down the path toward us, skipping along in notes, while the announcer with his practised English accent told us (I always believed) that we weren't quite up to snuff.

That is, the music did not quite fit; while the wheat board had as much to do with us, it seemed, as the end-of-the-day stock report, filed out to children, with spring trout in their hands, holding them up for a black-and-white picture against the backdrop of old spruce.

I think of this when I think of my home—whenever I am driving from Toronto back down through Quebec, with its solitude and its large farms, onto Highway 185, which is the worst highway in the country (so I've been told) and through the dark spruces of the

Plaster Rock Highway, where I've seen men stranded in the middle of the night and truckers unhitching their loads in solitude to make the iced-over hills in bitter cold. These were men I grew up with, a part of me, and characters for my novels—greatness to me could never be middle-class comfort, and could never be feminist angst— but it could/would always be both men and women. I thought Canada understood that, and in some ways the best of Canada did. On the home front our writers/journalists became obsessed not by rights of man but by attaining privileges for the privileged, and did not seem to know the difference . . . so great novels were called "bleak," and novels about middle-class society—novels of comfortable victimization that always proved a point for contented readers— were called "radical." Most of the men women writers wrote about back in the seventies and eighties weren't men I recognized; they did, however, fill a convenient slot in these progressive books, and in some way they must have been the talented men these women came to know as Canadian men. But their stance in the world was so often small and diminished by the books written.

Yet I realized as I got older that Canada wanted to be diminished. It wanted to lessen its role in the world, its obligation to the world, while still maintaining a voice in the world. One just might say this was the coward's way out. In this diminishing from 1960 forward, Canada lost much of its moral right, while shouting from the higher moral ground, usually against our nearest neighbour, the United States—and of course against British imperialism. I realized in a true way we existed at the pleasure of United States after 1964—and yet we thought we were morally above them most of the time.

Then Quebec's voice for independence came along when I was a young man.

So my country's focus changed almost 360 degrees. On a national scale after I was nineteen the trendiest needs were those of Quebec. I came to believe by 1972 that Quebec was in many ways a self-traumatized, self-obsessed adolescent, trying to hide at least a little bit of racist acne.

What I remember when I listened to the debates of the late sixties onward was the sham of it all—and the shame. The posturing of politicians showed that lack of subtlety in hauling the wool over our own eyes. This happened in two ways: English Canada must be sensitive to what French Quebec had suffered, while Quebec continually exhibited an intolerant ideological unawareness toward the rest of Canada that was not only accepted but supposedly understood.

And since the intellectuals formed their own class and not only framed the argument but were the only class of people who seemed to be allowed to discuss Canada, it became a one-sided dressing down of people who never had any say. Suddenly, by the time I was twenty those millions of us, who never had a say one way or the other, were told we no longer had a say. It was the first time I heard the name rednecks and bigots recklessly used against people I generally respected, and in the way those words were perceived were neither bigots nor rednecks.

Still the radio came to our out-of-the-way villages and houses, and told us things about ourselves almost none of us needed to hear. It was at that time, with 30 percent unemployment in my hometown, that I got a call from a friend in Montreal asking me if I had finally sensitized myself to Quebec and their quest for freedom. He was thrilled at the idea that he could now lecture me—and prevalent modern opinion would allow him to.

What was pertinent here was my answer; that is, he wanted me to beg him not to succeed. To show the proper amount of English shame.

But I did not play the game—from that moment on I simply said Quebec could go or stay; it made no difference to me because it was not up to me—it was up to them.

That is, after eleven years of asking him to give us a chance—of reiterating what the radio told me I must feel—I no longer had the inclination to care. They—that is, CBC—on the issue of what Canada was and what it needed no longer represented me. In some respects I didn't even know where that Canada was.

"If you do not watch it, we will go."

I was looking out the window at a numbing snow—my wife and I were literally down to our last twenty dollars.

"Goodbye," I said.

But that was in 1981—by then I was writing my fourth novel, which seemed so far removed from the world I was supposed to celebrate, his world in Montreal and most of any other world our TV told us about. I had caught on to the trick—and after I had I could never pretend I did not, even for my own well-being—and the trick was this: Canadians like me must agree with what others in urban media outlets promoted as Canada—and if we did not, we would never be as Canadian as they were. But the real secret was: even if we did agree, we would still have to apologize for who we were most of our lives. And I would not apologize or feel less than those who told me to, again.

In Canada by that time most of the trains had been replaced by jet travel, and the CBC promoted us not by speaking of us as a nation—but by telling us continually how we must be one. But even that stopped after a time. Though my feeling is they want me to understand that people like me have made some mistake; and sooner or later they will tell me it has to be corrected, for my own good.

Over the years, many of my friends left my province to go out West to work. They had to, to keep their families alive. And now Alberta is feeling pressure from those from the centre of our country who tell it continually they have done something wrong. The world changed, and Canada grew further and further away from who I was and am.

I still love it desperately, but I doubt, except in our glorious hockey, if we ever got it right. Many men and women have died for it, showing grace and courage under fire, knowing this tragic truth themselves.

Still, in the end, getting it right might be asking far too much. Though with all we've been through, and all we know, for the sake of our land, for the dreams we have, we all must, for those who come after us, continue to try.

1998

WE WALKED THE CAMINO

MY WIFE CAME WITH ME. AS ALWAYS. THE YEAR BEFORE, WHEN I had my first heart attack, she was waiting for me, and then the second, again she was there. Over my life she was there when my books were attacked or went out of print. She was there, too, when friends turned their back and I was alone.

Then I fell, off the back of my porch and hit my head—yes, I am a walking disaster. I always was. So for almost a month I tried to walk normally—or as normally as I could manage at the best of times. But I wobbled all over the place, had to hold on to things whenever I stood.

Finally I went to a doctor and then a neurologist.

Four vertebrae discs had pinched my spinal cord up at my neck, and it was bent like a curve ball. They needed to operate. The doctor, a very kind and good man, said there was a chance, slim though it was, that I would be paralyzed from the neck down. So it was my decision. Not a great one to have to make no matter how small that chance was.

She stayed with me, and when I woke after the three-hour operation, she was in the elevator:

Can he move his right arm, my sister had texted her. For my left arm was never much good.

I reached up and took her hand.

Yes, she texted back, *he can.*

Anyway, before that—after my second heart attack—we walked the Camino. The way of Saint James. The Apostle of Christ. Bringing his message to the world of Iberia. Thousands of people followed the way over the years—over the millennium. Thousands upon thousands of people have crossed the Pyrenees to walk the way of Saint James. One almost says, who am I not to do so. And so in 2014 the two of us went. You see, I have written about religion as it differs from spirituality—but she, my wife, was the one more spiritual, kinder, far more gentle than I. Far more gentle—in an ungentle world.

I had a dream when I was nine years old. In the dream I was walking up the old pathway that led from town to the Rocks—the section of town where I lived—and I stepped over a white stone. Afterward I searched everywhere for that white stone—never found it, really— but I began after I was married to pick my wife white stones off the beaches I visited and bring them home.

STARTING OUT

There are as many reasons for doing this as there are people doing it. For some it is simply the idea of making it across the Pyrenees from France to Spain and travelling all the way to Santiago de Compostela. Which is over five hundred miles. Others bicycle it, wearing Spandex shorts. Others do it as if it is a marathon. Some might do it as a lark. I might have done it only to see how far along it I could get. But all of us see things on the journey that are bound to astound—to make us realize—well, perhaps make us realize that there is a God that does exist after all. No it is not an unusual observation. I'm not trying to make it one. It is just that so many things have happened in my life, or to my life that I can no longer deny.

Walking up the mountain the first day, the sheets of flowers and crops in the fields miles apart from one another, the houses and villages resting below us, the sun in the wide grand sky, the French Mirage fighter jets swooping across the valley almost at eye level. It was hard walking, almost straight up to the heavens. But we made it to the *albergue* just before supper.

The second day we befriended three open-hearted, wonderful Australian women. So we walked over the top of the mountain with them, high in the world, with the scent of fresh snow and nearing the Spanish side in midday.

Coming down late in the afternoon—having been taken partway across the mountain by a tiny but rugged French-Vietnamese guide who had adopted us—to the Spanish monastery. To the sunlight diminishing in the sky against monastery windows six or seven centuries old, to the Australian women ecstatic that they had seen snow in the mountains, to the rows of hedges and flowers of northern Spain. To dinner and a late mass—where so many people, Catholic and Protestant, attended—suddenly people, affluent or not, from Ireland, the Netherlands, Australia, the States, England, Canada and many places besides, simply—*simply* is the best word—crowded in to hear the gospel—because for some reason, no matter how far one has strayed or how slight the belief, the truth of the gospel is still immediate and ever present.

I thought of the cross put up in honour of the two Swiss men who had fallen from the mountain and had died the year before.

THE DARLING OF JAPANESE DOCUMENTARY TV

My wife asked me to go on this pilgrimage. Without her I would not have gone. She became the darling of Japanese documentary television for a while. A petite woman with a knapsack and a cap, with compassionate blue eyes and greying black hair, trudging along beside me. As she had done most of her life.

We were followed by a Japanese television crew wondering why we did this. But you see, they pray, too, just as I said in my book *God Is.*; everyone in the world does, even those who call those who pray "hypocrites." I have been called that enough, by people who know my rather outlandish life—nor do I blame them one bit.

When the film crew saw us, walking up toward a copse of trees on the third day, suddenly we, the oldest people on the journey at that time, two people in their sixties, were surrounded by cameras and microphones—the kind of things journalists do.

"Are you tired—can you keep up—why are you doing this?"

And then the most personal of questions, almost as personal as a question about sexual preference: "Are you religious."

"No. Yes. I am not sure. Sometimes."

The interviewer was young enough to be our granddaughter.

So she and her interpreter and her cameraman followed us, along the copse, through to a roadway and up a long white stairway. Every time we turned around to see her, she would smile timidly and bow. We liked her a good deal. They stayed at the same *albergue*.

Then they followed us into the dormitory that night, where they watched my wife wrap her sore feet. Then they filmed me looking concerned at her toes. We did not see the documentary, but I am sure she made a splash.

PEGGY

Without her I would not be alive. I would simply have drunk myself to death in my thirties. There is no question that is what I would have done.

My wife was born in 1950 in the kitchen of her house. Her mother was left a widow with nine children. One Christmas Peggy got a tiny jar of fingernail polish, for the doll she got the Christmas before.

I never heard her complain about poverty, call herself a victim, demand more—demand an apology from anyone—even from one who betrayed and hurt her.

She never partook in feminist angst. But she learned to fly a plane at twenty-six. She never marched for freedom, but she rides a Harley. She never spoke about being equal, but she could handle a horse, and paint a house, and fix a stove, and she didn't get a master's or a doctorate to get a job that would reinforce her bias.

She doesn't always remember the characters in my books, or why I write the way I do; can't get through Henry James—not sure of when certain wars happened or why; but she can remember conversations and incidents that happened twenty-five years before, who ordered what at what restaurant on trips long past; took care of children—not only her own—with deep love. And I remembered all of this as she sat down on a rock in the middle of nowhere, and cut some bread and cheese for us, and handed me a drink of water, telling me to take my pills. Here we were six thousand miles from home, and the tender way she smiled she might have easily been sitting along the banks of the Bartibog when we fished it as kids. I suppose in that way, the way she accepts who it is she is, I am in awe.

THOUGHTS ALONG THE ROAD

We crossed over northern Spain, saw where Hemingway might have fished. I stopped and listened to the rapids. A tributary of the Ebro, and I realized I, too, might like to cast a fly across a certain part of that water. There would be trout there I decided—in the pocket just below the rip, where the rock just broke water.

I have fly-fished a lot in my life and realize why Hemingway loved it. I fished with many who would have put Hemingway to shame fishing, but so what. I think there is something noble about the rural life if handled right—and I thought, too, of the Spanish Civil War—one of the great battles was fought along the Ebro, I think.

Hemingway, a Catholic, like Fitzgerald was as tormented about his Catholicism as I was and am at times. At its moral stringency and priestly pretense, its Vatican opulence. And the terrible cover-ups of crime. But still he could not put it behind him. Ever. For there is something else Catholicism carries in its genes, beyond all of that, beyond all of that—a grasp, a grasp of infinite truth.

I remembered, too, that this is where Orwell began to have second thoughts about communist thuggery, when he came here to fight Franco. What amazes me about a man so clever is that he had to come this far to find out. Still, I doubt he walked the Camino. He hated Catholicism in a very traditional British way. You could almost see him sitting about in a common room, in tweeds, mocking it all.

Hemingway might have wanted to walk the Camino. Of course he was in Pamplona with the bulls, drinking in a bar Peg and I got to after a week.

As we sat in the huge bar, Hemingway's favourite, I thought Ernest in many respects got a bad rap by people who would never in their lives be able to write "A Clean, Well-Lighted Place."

I wondered if they met ever, Hemingway and Orwell—and what they would have said to each other. Perhaps that they had the same naïve misconception about Stalin and the sanctity of the left.

I also thought of something else. Villon was exiled from Paris in 1463. Seeing the thickness of the ancient medieval walls of Pamplona, I realized that for Monsieur Villon, exile was a death sentence.

MEETING PEOPLE

For the most part I'm against it. I was making a singular journey— not for any reason except in hope. I was free from booze for over ten years when an accident and a short prescription with painkillers put me on the road to addiction again. An addiction to opioids that almost destroyed my life. I was able to stop cold turkey. By 2014 I was off them for over ten years. But it had been hell for my family and me. That is why Peg asked me to do this. I was making this journey in atonement. I know a lot about that, and as much about addiction as anyone. There is not an addict that I don't feel some affinity with, in some way, on this or any other journey into the dark.

I met at least a dozen others doing the exact same thing. One gentleman carrying a heavy backpack in penance said to me, "I am trying to make up for a life of mistakes and terrible decisions."

"Yes—" I said. "Join the club. Many of us here are here for a simi-lar reason."

Another was in tears because he had left his snakes behind and missed them.

"Ah, your snakes," I said. "How many snakes?"

"Twenty-seven," he said.

"Ah," I said, "twenty-seven—well, when you get home, they'll be waiting."

We met a British woman who was lost. We shared our last bottle of water with her, and she followed us down the right path to the small village. She had been wandering along the road, unable to speak the language, crying. Like the Australians before her, there was an almost instant bond. But there was a bond with the Dutch girls, too, and the German lady—and the Australian man we had supper with. Most of the people were very kind.

We met other Canadians, as well. Most of them were thirty years younger than us, but not all—a good number were men and women in their fifties.

We walked by forts built a thousand years ago by the Knights Templar guarding pilgrims who were walking the Camino, and who were in danger of being robbed and murdered. Tiny little stone-and-mortar structures in vast fields, left to history and the weather. State of the art back then, with their turrets and crow's nest.

We had mass at a monastery with a heavy bronze cross on the altar that was carried over the mountains by German pilgrims in AD 900. Drank from water fountains that have supplied pilgrims since 1033. Maybe this journey was in someway coming home.

SO THEN THIS HAPPENED

We were in a small *albergue* after a long day. My feet had had it. They were torn up very badly. I had lost most of my toenails, and the blisters were such it was agony to walk. Peggy's feet had healed, and for the first time on the journey she was walking ahead of me, waiting for me to catch up. The Australian women had tried to help my toes earlier. Big Sue, who was five feet eleven inches, and Little Sue, who was five feet one inch, friends since kindergarten, and their friend, a woman whose name I regrettably forget, who was a nurse. But it was not to be. I had made a fundamental mistake. I had bought a brand-new pair of sneakers the day before I left for Spain. I knew I was taking a chance doing so, and now I was paying for that.

We were at an *albergue* by four in the afternoon, put into a room with six other pilgrims. The room was small, with eight bunk beds. When Peg and I entered, a young Spaniard standing in his undershorts, and seeing Peg—not prepared to see a woman walk in—started to shake and bark. He continued to bark and two other young Spanish men came in to speak with him. It was not that other women were not in this room—an Australian woman and a Japanese woman were there, as well. But they had put their packs down and gone out. So the man thought he was alone at that moment and had taken that chance to have a shower. Seeing Peg startled him.

"Look," I said to Peg, "I have not slept in forty-eight hours, my feet are driving me crazy—if he continues to bark, I will have another sleepless night—we might have to change *albergues*—"

"Well—just wait and see," she said.

So that night we went down to supper and sat at the large table with those men. It was Holy Week. They were from Barcelona. I noticed the men he was with for the first time. All my life I have been around tough men—grown up with them. So I knew these fellows were the real deal. We spoke about the Camino, and Canada, and how cold it was (that is the starting point for many conversations), and that someone had a relative who worked in Thunder Bay and did I know him. They noticed my tattoo and asked what it was. Then they showed theirs. But that is not the point—the point is, it was Holy Week. And these men, tough as nails, had brought their good friend who had Tourette syndrome along to walk with them—hoping for a miracle—not for them—no, they did not want anything for themselves, but for him. Naïve, well—no more than anyone. Compassionate—yes. Very compassionate. Innocent, too. So I no longer considered changing anything. They would head off to the next town early the next morning, the three of them, two earnestly hoping for the one, and I never saw them again.

That day as we walked, we came to a long pathway leading down to a village in the sun. The pathway was covered—with thousands upon thousands of white stones—the very shape and size of the white stone I had stepped over in my dream when I was nine years old.

LOURDES

I was kicked off the Camino. Yes, I was. Not by the law, or religious edict, but by a nice doctor:

"*No camino no más—por uno año,*" she said. And she pointed her finger at me sternly and wagged it. Then her assistant poured some yellow liquid over my feet and wrapped them.

She said I would begin to lose them if I kept going. Or at least part of them—perhaps starting with my toes and working back so by the end of the trip I would be walking on my ankles.

I felt bad, because Peg was coming into her own. I had cut back my sneakers so my toes stuck out, yet to no avail.

"If it was only one or two toes," I said to Peg, "then you know—well, I would continue—but as you heard—all my toes—I would have probably zero toes."

The clinic was going to charge me ninety euros, but the doctor came out to reception and said, "No, *señor*, it is on *España*—good luck."

I guess everything happens for a reason. I took a picture of Peg at the arch over the pathway where we would continue to walk if and when we got back. Then, since it was Holy Week, we headed to Lourdes. The place of Saint Bernadette, of the Immaculate Conception, of the Virgin in the Grotto. Who believes that silly stuff? I do. At least at times. There are days I miss, but most days I do. So curse me. But there was a moment when you realized how the corporate world always takes over—everything in Lourdes was for sale. All was glitter and gloss, and the message was lost in lights and dazzle.

We walked down to the grotto, and that is where in that little place we were at peace. There were no Lourdes lighters, or prayer beads, or candle holders. There was just the place where the little girl knelt when she saw the vision. And what horrible trouble she got into when everyone told her she did not see it. That she was a liar. That her family was disreputable. Her father in jail.

Just like the children in Fatima in 1917, she was harassed and mocked. Yet she kept going back to the grotto by the stream, listening to the beautiful lady no one else could see. Now there is a magnificent church above the grotto, built by those religious men and women who had first tormented and mocked her. Seems that happens quite a bit.

You see, I dedicated a book to her—not to Saint Bernadette, but to *Her*—when I was fighting opioids and I said to her, "If you help me get off these damn things, because it was a prescription that got me on them, so unlike my booze years, it wasn't my fault (I was very careful not to say "it was your fault") and it is causing havoc with those I love and would give my life for, and everything so—why, if you do—well then—okay, I will *dedicate this book* to you."

I said that kind of on the spur of the moment. But I knew *she* wouldn't forget. So I did dedicate the book to her. I suppose it was like Nowlan dedicating a book to Saint Jude when he was going through his cancer operations.

We walked back to our hotel later. Peg asked me if there were miracles anymore. For it seemed the world didn't believe in them. I thought of the men with their friend with Tourette's. I thought of the hundreds of men and women we met along the Camino. I saw a young boy pushing his younger sister in a wheelchair up toward the grotto in the late afternoon. Yes, one could lessen themselves and mock it.

"Oh yes," I said. "There must be—the miracle of belief. And what do we know of miracles—they might happen every day."

When we came into our hotel, one of the hotel clerks motioned to me and said the CBC from Toronto was trying to contact me.

We went to our room, and the phone rang. A producer from *As It Happens* said that Carol Off wanted to speak with me, because my good friend Alistair MacLeod had died that day.

It was Easter Sunday. The book I had dedicated to *her* I had also dedicated to him, to Alistair.

The dedication reads: "For Alistair MacLeod, and for Our Lady of Light."

Ten minutes before, we were sitting near the grotto where Bernadette told at first her parents and then the world that SHE had appeared.

I am sure Alistair never knew I would be at Lourdes the day he died. Of course neither did I. Not in my wildest dreams.

I am almost positive someone else probably did.

2017

THANKS TO

My wife Peggy, my sons John and Anton, my editor Tim Rostron.

ABOUT THE AUTHOR

DAVID ADAMS RICHARDS is one of Canada's preeminent writers. His recent novels include *Mary Cyr* and *Principles to Live By*, as well as *Crimes Against My Brother* and *Incidents in the Life of Markus Paul*, both of which were longlisted for the Scotiabank Giller Prize. Among his other novels, *Mercy Among the Children* won the Giller Prize and was shortlisted for the Governor General's Literary Award and the Trillium Award. Richards has written four bestselling books of nonfiction: *Lines on the Water*, *God Is*, *Facing the Hunter* and *Hockey Dreams*. In 2017, David Adams Richards was appointed to the Senate of Canada on the advice of Prime Minister Justin Trudeau.

A NOTE ABOUT THE TYPE

Murder and Other Essays is set in Monotype Dante, a modern font family designed by Giovanni Mardersteig in the late 1940s. Based on the classic book faces of Bembo and Centaur, Dante features an italic, which harmonizes extremely well with its roman partner. The digital version of Dante was issued in 1993, in three weights and including a set of titling capitals.